TATTING PATTERNS

Julia E. Sanders

DOVER PUBLICATIONS, INC.
NEW YORK

PUBLISHER'S NOTE

The crochet cotton referred to in the text is still available in most of the sizes recommended, although the names "Cordonnet," "Cordonnet Special," "Cordichet" and "Kord-net" are no longer used. Pearl Cotton can also be used for tatting, and several thread companies now manufacture special Tatting Cotton which can be purchased wherever needlework supplies are sold.

Coronation Cord is no longer available, but soutache braid makes a workable substitute.

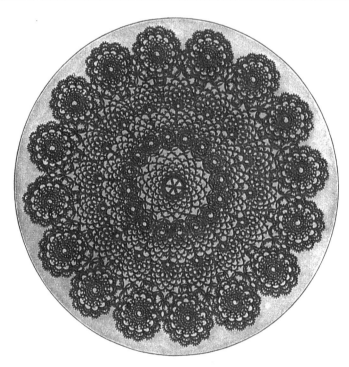

FIG. 1. CENTREPIECE—TATTING WITH CORONATION CORD.
SEE DOILIES TO MATCH ON PAGE 14, AND DIRECTIONS ON PAGE 10

This Dover edition, first published in 1977, is an unabridged republication of the work first published by The Priscilla Publishing Company in 1915 under the title *The Priscilla Tatting Book No. 2. A collection of Beautiful and Useful Patterns with Directions for Working.*

International Standard Book Number

ISBN-13: 978-0-486-23554-7
ISBN-10: 0-486-23554-8

Manufactured in the United States by LSC Communications
23554824   2018
www.doverpublications.com

Explanation of Stitches

DOUBLE STITCH (d s). Two half stitches made with the shuttle, forming one stitch.

RING (r). The required number of double stitches made with the shuttle thread only, and drawn up into a ring.

CHAIN (ch). A scallop or cord made with the ball thread, on the shuttle thread, not drawn up into a ring.

PICOT (p). A loop left between stitches; (l p) a long picot; (sm p) a very small picot.

SLIP STITCH (sl st). Thread passed under the work to the next point.

JOSEPHINE KNOT. A ring formed of single stitches, like the first half of a d s; it may be of four to twelve stitches.

JOIN. A loop drawn through a picot, shuttle passed through it, and thread drawn tightly. Or with the ball thread; or threads tied around.

CONTINUOUS THREAD. Thread unbroken between shuttle and ball.

REVERSE. Turn the work, and continue as before, but in an opposite direction.

THE TERM, 3 ps 2 d s between, of any number, means, as many d s before and after as between.

SETS OF STITCHES (sts). 4-4, or other numbers; are single stitches of the stated number, like the first half of a d s; then the same number of single stitches, like the last half of a d s; this is one set of stitches.

Directions

Modern Tatting.—The new or Modern Tatting differs in general style and appearance from that with which we are all familiar. The chief charm of the old tatting lay in its fineness, and in the feathery daintiness lent by the use of many picots; that of the new lies rather in its conventionality of design, its durability and its closeness of texture, which render it useful for many purposes for which the old was unfit. New materials, stitches, terms, and directions are used in the Modern Tatting.

FIG. 2. EDGING. SEE PAGE 4

In stitches, besides those described on page 3, are several new variations of old stitches. As *double rings; shell picot,* a very loose Josephine knot of five stitches, made with only the shuttle thread, generally at the joining of a chain to the row before, but may be on other parts of the chain. *Slip stitch,* may be done neatly at the back of the work, with a fine crochet-hook, carrying the thread back of stitches or through them; by running through chains; by sewing, or in various other ways to suit the situation.

In the directions for Tatted Cords, page 28, will be found several new cords which may be used in numerous ways to furnish pleasing variety and new figures in tatting.

A worker who well merits the title of Lady Superior in the art of Tatting, has given the following valuable hints, which will add greatly to the perfection of the work, if carried out.

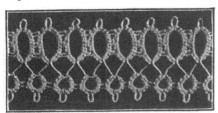

FIG. 3. BEADING. SEE PAGE 4

"In making tatting use a continuous thread—unbroken between ball and shuttle —as much as possible.

"Slip stitch from one row to another when convenient.

"When using continuous thread, a second ball for refilling the shuttle will avoid cutting the ball thread.

"After tying the ends it will often make the work neater to sew them with very fine thread.

"If the edge of the work seems too full it will press out flat and look much better than if it must be stretched.

"With a large piece of work it is well to press occasionally while making, and all work should be thoroughly pressed when finished.

"To press, place the work right side down, on flannel, pull well into shape with the fingers; with a wet cloth over the work, then a dry cloth, press with quite a hot iron, remove first cloth after a little, continue pressing until work is thoroughly dry."

The old saying about "tricks in all trades," applies in one sense to tatting. There are so many new ways, makeshifts, and ingenious devices, for gaining dexterity, perfection, and beauty of design. One worker rarely uses the ring, instead laps and joins the chain into a ring. Another rarely uses the chain, but says: "Whenever possible I leave a thread and *crochet* over it. The result is about the same."

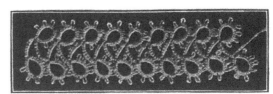

FIG. 4. INSERTION. SEE PAGE 4

We hear much of "the new way of tatting," which many have long known as the only way. It is, passing the shuttle between the first and second fingers of the left hand, instead of around the whole hand, and is much more rapid.

Materials.—Where the words "crochet cotton" are used in the text of this book, the cotton referred to is the hard-twisted cotton known by such names as Cordonnet, Cordonnet Special, Cordichet, Kord-net, etc., which can be purchased wherever needlework supplies are sold.

The numbers of crochet cotton generally used are, for very small edgings, Nos. 70 to 100; other edgings, Nos. 50 and 60, also for other fine work; from Nos. 3 to 30 for towels, and very coarse work.

FIG 5. EDGING. SEE PAGE 4

Figure 2. Edging. — Begin with the leaflets at left of a daisy. R 9 d s, p, 5 d s, p, 14 d s. R 14 d s, p, 5 d s, p, 9 d s. Ch 16 d s, turn. DAISY. *Ring 1*— 10 d s, join 1st p of 1st r, 4 d s, p, 4 d s, p, 10 d s. *Ring 2*—10 d s, join last r, 8 d s, p, 10 d s. Join all rings. Repeat ring 2, twice; r 1, twice; then r 2, omitting the last p, turn. Ch 15, join upper leaflet; ch 10 d s, p, 11 d s, turn. Repeat first leaflet, join 1st p to 6th r of the daisy. Repeat r and ch 16 d s. Join 1st r of daisy to first leaflet, and 5th r of first daisy.

Figure 3. Beading. — But one thread is used. R 3 ds, 3 p 3 d s between, turn, leave a short thread; r 7 p 3 d s between (bet), turn, leave same length of thread; r 3 p 3 d s bet, join first p to last p of the small ring, turn; r 7 p 3 d s bet, join first three p to the last three of the large r.

Figure 4. Insertion. — Ring 4 d s, 7 p 3 d s between (bet), 4 d s; ch 7 d s; repeat r on the other side; ch 7 d s; reverse, r 4 d s, join 4th p of the first r, 6 p 3 d s bet, 4 d s. Repeat on alternate sides.

FIG. 6. EDGING. SEE PAGE 4

Figure 5. — Make a r of 7 d s, p, 7 d s; ch encircling it, 5 d s, p, 5 d s, p, 9 d s, p, 9 d s, p, 5 d s, p, 5 d s; join base of ring; ch 5 d s, 3 p, 3 d s between (bet), 5 d s; r 5 d s, join 1st p of ch, 2 d s, p, 5 d s; ch 5 d s, 3 p 3 d s bet, 5 d s.

Figure 6. — Make a large r with 4 d s, p, 4 d s, 3 p 1 d s between (bet), 4 d s, p, 4 d s, p, 9 d s, p, 9 d s, close. Ch 6 d s, p, 3 d s, p, 3 d s, p, 3 d s, join p bet the two 9 d s. R 3 d s, join last p, 4 d s, p, 4 d s, p, 3 d s. Ch 3 d s, join last p of r, 3 d s, p, 3 d s, p, 6 d s, join p at top of large r, ch 3 d s. Repeat as in cut.

Figure 7. — Make all of the picots small. Begin with the 4-ringed figure. R 4 d s, p, 4 d s, turn, ch 4 d s, 3 p 2 d s between, 4 d s; r 4 d s, join p of first r, 4 d s. Repeat ch and r twice, join rings in p of the first r, making a scallop of 4 r and 3 ch. Repeat r opposite the last. Repeat ch and r twice, join rings in p of first r, making a scallop with 3 r and 2 ch, ch 5 d s; r 3 d s, join mid-p of 4-ringed figure, 4 d s, p, 4 d s, p, 3 d s; ch 5 d s. Repeat the 3-ringed

figure, join 1st p to the other 3-ringed figure. Repeat from beginning.

Figure 8. — Large r 5 d s, p, 5 d s, 3 p 1 d s between (bet), 5 d s, p, 5 d s, p, 9 d s, p, 9 d s. Ch 6 d s, p, 3 d s, p, 3 d s, p, 3 d s. Trefoil, 3 d s, join last p of ch, 3 d s, 2 p 3 d s bet, 3 d s. Centre r, 3 d s, join last p, 4 d s, 3 p 1 d s bet, 4 d s, p, 3 d s. Repeat first r and join. Ch 3 d s, join last p of r. 3 d s, p, 3 d s, p, 6 d s, join p at top of r. Ch 2 d s; r 3 d s, p, 3 d s, 3 p 1 d s bet, 3 d s, p, 3 d s, ch 2 d s.

Figure 9. Insertion. — R 5 d s, 3 p 5 d s between, 5 d s; ch 6 d s, p, 6 d s, repeat the r, join 1st ring; ch 8 d s, p, 8 d s. Repeat rings and chains, joining as in the cut.

Figure 10. — Repeat the large r and ch of Fig. 6. R 3 d s, join p of ch, 3 d s, 6 p 1 d s between (bet),

FIG. 7. EDGING. SEE PAGE 4

7 d s, join ring; r 7 d s, join last p, 5 p 1 d s between, 3 d s, p, 3 d s, join r; ch 3 d s, join last p, 3 d s, p, 3 d s, p, 6 d s, join p in top of large r; ch 2 d s; r 6 d s, p, 6 d s; ch 2 d s.

Figure 11. Insertion. — This is made with two shuttles. First shuttle, ch 1 d s, p, * 5 d s, p, 5 d s; second shuttle, r 5 d s, p, 5 d s, p, 2 d s, p, 2 d s, p, 5 d s, p, 5 d s; first shuttle, ch 5 d s, p, 5 d s, join to first p made; second shuttle, 7 d s; first shuttle, r 5 d s, p, 5 d s, p, 2 d s, p, 5 d s, p, 5 d s; second shuttle, ch 7 d s. Repeat from *, joining together the rings of the three rows.

Figure 12. Insertion. — Ch 7 d s, p, 7 d s, r 3 p 3 d s between (bet), ch 7 d s, p, 7 d s, r 9 p, 3 d s bet. Repeat. For use as insertion, make a second row of edging and join the picot to the first row.

Figure 13. Trimming. — Make clover leaf (c l), 4 d s, p, 3 d s, p, 2 d s, p, 2 d s, p, 3 d s, p, 4 d s, make 3 r joined at 1st p; ch 6 d s, p, 6 d s, small r 3 d s, p, 2 d s, p, 2 d s, p, 3 d s; ch, 6 d s, p, 6 d s; c l joining mid-p of first r to mid-p of last r of the c l before. Repeat from beginning until there

FIG. 8. EDGING. SEE PAGE 4

4

are seven c l and six small r; repeat ch r ch, twice; then c l, joining mid-p of first r to last of the small r; mid-p of 2d r to side p of first small r, and mid-p of 3d r join to mid-p of first c l. Ch, small r ch and a c l of which join mid-p of first r to the joining of the two former c l. Repeat until 5 c l form a half circle, then reverse the c l, joining the first to the last one of the circle before. Repeat.

Figure 14. Trimming for Hat-band. — Use No. 40 crochet cotton, white or écru. Make a ch, 5 p 2 d s between (bet), 12 d s; r, 2 d s, 7 p 2 d s bet, 5 d s; leave a short thread; r 5 d s, join last p, 4 p 2 d s bet, 5 d s; r 5 d s, join, 6 p 2 d s bet, 5 d s; repeat 2d r, then 1st r. Ch 12 d s, join, 6 p, 2 d s bet, 9 d s; r 4 d s, join 3d p of last r, 4 d s, p, 4 d s; r 4 d s, join, 3 p 2 d s bet, 4 d s; r 4 d s, join, 4 d s, p, 4 d s; ch 9 d s, join. Make another row and join as in the cut.

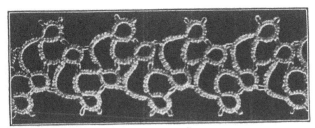

FIG. 9. INSERTION. SEE PAGE 4

Figure 15. Trimming for Hat-rim. — Use Crochet cotton No. 40, white or écru. Make a r 4 d s, 6 p 2 d s between (bet), 4 d s; ch 4 d s, 11 p, 4 d s; turn, r, 9 p 2 d s bet; ch 2 d s, 4 p, join 2d p of first r, 6 p 2 d s bet, 4 d s; r, 3 p, 3 d s bet; r, 3 d s, join last r, 3 d s, join 1st p of large centre r, 3 d s, p, 3 d s; repeat r, completing a trefoil; ch, 2 d s, 11 p 2 d s bet, 4 d s. Repeat trefoils, joining the one before, and every other p of the central r. Make 5 chains around the trefoils. Join the next outer ch to the 1st p of the first ch, the large outer r to an inner ch, and the figures, by 3d p of adjoining chains.

Figure 16. Trimming. — Make a ch of 6 d s, 2 p 3 d s between (bet), 8 d s, p, 6 d s; r, 12 d s, join end of the ch, 8 d s, p, 3 d s; r 3 d s, join last p, 8 d s, p, 8 d s, p, 4 d s; ch 9 d s; r 4 d s, join last p, 8 d s, p, 12 d s; very close to last, r, 12 d s, p, 8 d s, p, 4 d s; ch 9 d s; r 4 d s, join last p, 8 d s, p, 8 d s, p, 3 d s; r 3 d s, join last p, 8 d s, p, 12 d s; ch 6 d s, p, 8 d s, 2 p 3 d s bet, 6 d s, join p of last r. Repeat. Make a second row and join to the first, as in the cut.

Figure 17. Insertion. — This is made with two

FIG. 10. EDGING. SEE PAGE 4

FIG. 11. INSERTION. SEE PAGE 4

shuttles and two spools. Make a clover leaf (c l); first r 8 d s, p, 6 d s, p, 8 d s, p, 6 d s; second r 6 d s, join last p, 8 d s, p, 8 d s, p, 6 d s; third r 6 d s, join, 8 d s, p, 6 d s, p, 8 d s. Join the second thread to the 2d p of the 1st r; ch 8 d s, p, 12 d s, p, 6 d s, join mid-p of 2d r; ch 6 d s, p, 12 d s, p, 8 d s, join mid-p of 3d r, ch 6 d s; repeat c l, then with the first shuttle, repeat ch around c l, and a c l.

Figure 18. Silk Dress Trimming. — This can be made with crochet or purse silk. Begin with small r and ch between (bet) the large figures. R 3 p 3 d s bet; ch 9 d s, p, 9 d s; r 10 d s, 6 p 2 d s bet, 10 d s; ch, 5 p 2 d s bet, join 1st p in large r; * ch 6 d s; r 3 p 3 d s bet; ch 6 d s; join 2d p in large r; * repeat from * to * four times, joining rings together; ch 5 p 4 d s bet, join base of large r. Repeat ch and small r. If these figures are joined to the small r bet, the trimming will be firmer, and still more so if the adjoining rings at points of the figures are joined. *Upper row*—R 3 p 3 d s bet; ch 9 d s, join ch of first row at p after the small r, 9 d s; clover leaf of rings 3 p 5 d s bet, joined by first p; repeat ch, joining next p of first row.

Figure 19. Opera Bag. *Materials.* — Ecru crochet cotton No. 5, coronation cord (see Fig. 19½), one yard of ribbon, six in. wide, and 1½ yds. of fancy braid.

Join the thread to the cord; ch 3 d s, p, 3 d s; join cord, ch 3 d s, p, 3 d s; r 7 p 3 d s between (bet).

FIG. 12. INSERTION. SEE PAGE 4

Repeat rings and chains, joining the cord until there are eight of each. Join last ch to 2d p of last r; ch 3 d s, p, 3 d s, join cord, 3 d s, p, 3 d s, sm p. Repeat ch then r, joining 2d p to the sm p of ch, and 4th p to mid-p of last r. Continue up, as on the first side, joining rings by mid-ps. *Second row*— Chains and rings as first row, but reversed. After the r at turn of the end, ch 3 d s; r 5 p, 3 d s bet, join mid-p to corner next the nearest r of the first row, ch 3 d s. Repeat r, two ch, 2 r, short ch of 3 d s; r joined; short ch, then repeat rings and chains to the top. *Third row*—Turn ch back, join 2d p of last r, ch of 5 p, join same r, 6th p, bar of

5

3 d s, join 2d p of next r; repeat until the corner, then add four r of 3 p, with bars of 3 d s on each side, to fill spaces at the bottom; and continue up the side. *Fourth row*—Is of chains of 8 p and bars of 3 d s only. TATTED COILS FOR CORNERS.—With continuous thread; hold doubled end of thread in left thumb and finger, ch 4 d s, p, draw shuttle thread very close; continue with a p at every 3d d s. Draw close to form coil as made, and make 50 p. Sew on the wrong side. Crocheted balls are fastened by cords under the coils. BALLS.—Ch 4, join. In the ring make 10 double crochet (d), next row, 2 d in each d, making 20 d, 3 rows plain, then d in every other d, making 10 d. Stuff with cotton and close by making d in every other d. Crochet a ch cord of the length required.

To MAKE BAG.—Cut from linen canvas two pieces to fit tatting section one-half inch smaller, except at top. Cover these pieces with silk, turn edge of silk over canvas, and baste in place. Turn down two inches at each end of ribbon for heading. Gather remaining length on both edges. Sew gathered edges around sides and bottom of silk-covered sections. Blindstitch tatting section to silk-covered centres, letting last row tatting scallop overlap gathers in ribbon.

To LINE BAG.—Lay bag flat. Cut two pieces silk, size and shape of bag without the heading, seam to-

FIG. 13. TRIMMING. SEE PAGE 4

gether, tack inside bag, gather both ribbon and lining where they meet at top of bag. Let braid run across top of tatting section for finish, fastening ends under coils, as also the handles.

Figures 20-21. Yoke.—Use one ball of No. 80 crochet cotton and two shuttles. Tie shuttle threads together, using one thread as from a ball, ch 9 d s, p, 9 d s, p, until the ch is a little longer than the width of the yoke. Turn, with second shuttle make ring 3 d s, called a shell picot (s p), ch 4 d s, s p, 4 d s, join to last p of foundation ch; continue with 4 d s, s p, 4 d s, s p, 4 d s, join to next p of foundation ch. Continue the length of foundation ch. After joining to the end of ch, turn work *around*, not over, and continue as before, noticing that at the edges after work is turned a ch with 3 sp is made. Join the ch of the rows through the loop of former row as in crocheting (see detail, Fig. 21).

Figure 22. Wild Rose Spray of Black Crochet Silk.—The stems and parts of roses and buds are made in the tatted cord effect, in sets of stitches (see explanation, page 3).

ROSE.—With continuous thread. Leave a p at beginning, work 13 p 2 d s between (bet); form r by joining p left at beginning. Work six small petals around this r, of 6 sets, 4-4 sts each; join each

FIG. 14. TRIMMING FOR HAT-BAND. SEE FIG. 15, AND PAGE 5

second p around ring. *Second row of petals;* 5 d s, 12 small p, 3 d s bet, 5 d s, join each of the remaining ps on r. Work sets of 4-4 sts for stem to required length. To avoid ends make the stem first with continuous thread, and work on the rose after stem is made. Sew ends under the rose.

ROSE-BUD. — Begin buds without ends and at centre of point of bud. Leaving p at beginning, work 7 sets 4-4 sts with a p at beginning and centre of each set. *Centre of bud;* leaving a p; 27 d s, join p at beginning of bud; p 27 d s, join p. Work 12 sets 4-4 sts, join p left in last row at point of bud, work cluster of 5 long ps, 1 d s between, join at same p. Work 12 sets 4-4 sts, join at beginning of this row. Work 15 d s, form small loop at base of bud, by joining again in same place. Cross small loop and proceed with stem by sets of 4-4 sts. This makes the largest bud. Smaller ones are made with 6 sets 4-4 sts in centre, omitting the picots and working enough d s in first row, and sets of sts in second row, to make the shape desired, leave but 3 long p at end, shape the bud with fingers as made. Make stem of buds and roses from 2 to 4 inches in length.

LEAVES are begun at centre point of leaf, and made the same as buds, except having but one row around centre stem, and are wholly of sets of stitches and graduated in size to suit. Cut the silk after each leaf. Wind a little silk on shuttle, work leaf and 2 sets 4-4 sts after leaf. Cut threads, leaving about 2 inches; wind again for next leaf. Repeat twice; then make 6 sets sts for stem. Join a leaf to stem of this one at point of working; work 2 sets over the threads of the added leaf. Add the other leaf to opposite side of stem, and work over those ends in same manner. After a few sets of stitches the loose ends may be cut close to stem, this makes a cluster of leaves.

FIG. 15. TRIMMING FOR HAT-RIM. SEE FIG. 14, AND PAGE 5

The ends of the upper part are all brought together and sewed firmly, then fastened under rose at centre of spray. The rest sewed at the bottom, then wound smoothly with the silk.

FIG. 16. TRIMMING. SEE PAGE 5

Figure 23. Trimming of Metal Thread.—The metal thread is used from the ball, and hides the shuttle thread of crochet cotton. Commence in centre of a figure. Ch p, 3 d s, 8 p 2 d s between (bet); curl in a r, with crochet-hook draw the metal thread back of the shuttle thread, through the 1st p, join, and draw closely. Ch 1 d s, 3 p 2 d s bet, 1 d s, join a p of r. Repeat around. At the end of the second row around the centre r, and opposite to its beginning, make a r for the lower end, of 4 d s, 5 p 3 d s bet, 4 d s, join. Continue, as before, to the opposite side of coil; repeat r. Continue around, join next figure to the right, by 2 p. Join the p before lower r; ch 3 p, 3 d s bet, join 2d p of r; ch 5 p, 3 d s bet, join 4th p of r; ch 3 p, 3 d s bet, join p after r. Continue; around the upper r repeat the 3 ch, and close at right side of the r. The end figures have added rings in centre of side chains, of 6 p each. *The last row* is around all of the figures. Wind cotton on the shuttle enough to finish this row without joining. (Though a join can be made very neatly by sewing and wrapping the thread around.) Joining left of upper chains, 1st p; ch 3 p, 3 d s between, join same ch, next p; ch 2 d s, p, 2 d s, join next p; 2 d s, p, 2 d s, join next p; ch 3 d s, p, 3 d s, skip one p, join; ch 3 d s, p, 3 d s, join next p but one; 2 d s, p, 2 d s, join next p, and repeat twice; ch 7 d s, join together the 2d p from joining, and corresponding p of next figure, 7 d s. Repeat around the figures.

Figure 24. Daisy Spray.—Use crochet silk. The daisies are made separately. With continuous thread, ch a short stem, of a p and ten or twelve sets of 4-4 sts. Ch 16 d s, 3 long p 2 d s between (bet), 16 d s. Form into a loop, crossing at its beginning, shuttle thread over, ball thread under the ch, work 2 d s, draw shuttle thread very tight and thus form the first petal. Make seven petals very close together,

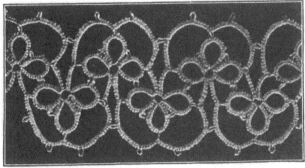

FIG. 17. INSERTION. SEE PAGE 5

join in a ring with first petal, and sew neatly to the stem, and a jet nailhead in the centre of each daisy. *Stem and leaves*—Ch 12 sets of 5-5 sts, p, 5 sets of 4-4 sts, reverse, 2 d s, 13 p 2 d s bet, draw tightly, join p, and form a leaf. Join a daisy by the p left on the stem. Make a set of 4-4 sts, then carry shuttle thread around the daisy to hold it firmly. Join daisies and leaves on opposite sides of the stem. Make the length of stem desired, of 5-5 sts, then another leaf and daisy. Leaving the p in the centre of a set of sts will bring it on the opposite side. Finish the spray with a daisy at the end of the stem, to give it a graceful finish.

Figure 25-32. Collar; Tatting Appliqué on Net.—Cut paper pattern, and baste net on it smoothly.

LATTICE WORK AROUND NECK. (See Fig. 30.)—Use No. 40 crochet cotton. With continuous thread, make p, 3 d s, 7 p 2 d s between (bet), 2 d s. Form small loop by crossing ch 1 d s, from beginning. Work 6 sets of 5-5 sts; ch 2 d s, 10 p 1 d s bet, 2 d s. Form small loop by crossing beginning of

FIG. 18. SILK DRESS TRIMMING. SEE PAGE 5

ch. Work 4 sets of 5-5 sts, cross ch of 5-5 sts first made, 2 sets from first loop. Work 2 sets 5-5 sts, make second loop on same side as first loop of 4 d s, 13 p 2 d s bet, 3 d s. Form large loop by crossing ch at beginning as before. Again 6 sets of 5-5 sts, loop of 2 d s, 10 p 1 d s bet, 2 d s. Form small loop as before. Work 2 sets 5-5 sts, join to first ch of 5-5 sts, 2 sets from first small loop of 10 p. Draw the ball thread under the ch, join with shuttle thread closely so that the ball thread is double around the ch, and shuttle thread straight through the joining; as always the shuttle thread above, ball thread under the work. Draw the ball thread through to the shuttle thread, work 2 sets of 5-5 sts, draw ball thread back which brings the two threads on opposite sides of work, as before. Cross the *last* long ch of 5-5 sts, work 2 sets 5-5 sts, which completes the pattern to a small loop on the side on which small and large loops alternate. Work lattice-work to reach around the neck. Baste this on, with the small loops even with the net. Work scallops around the outer edge of lattice-work, of 15 p 2 d s bet, join the small loops.

EDGING OF COLLAR.—Beginning with a p, ch 3 d s, 14 p, 1 d s bet, 3 d s, form loop, joining beginning of ch; work 4 sets 5-5 sts; repeat loop and ch.

plain d s for three rows, the last with a p after each
2d d s. Make seven coils with three rows of d s,
and eight with two rows. Sew rows together as
made.

FIG. 19½. CORONATION CORD, FULL SIZE, USED IN BAG,
FIG. 19

SMALL BUTTERFLY. (See Fig. 31.) —Use cotton No.
40. *Body*—Make p, and eight sets of 4-4 sts with short
ps at centre and longer ps between sets, then two sets
with only the short ps, turn, repeat, joining to the long
ps. At top join 1st p, then make 14 d s for loop
of head, join. *First Side Loop*—Join 3d p from top,
Make 19 sets of 5-5 sts with ps between sets, join end
of large loop. *Second Side Loop*—Join lower side of
first side loop—see Fig. 25; make 17 sets of 5-5
sts with ps, join
at same point
as last. This
forms the
larger part of
the wing on
one side. *The
smaller wing*—
Has thirteen
sets of 5-5 sts,
form in a loop,
join at same
point. This
completes one
side; repeat,
join the sides
together at
centre, sew the
ends closely
between the
wings, to be
covered by the
body. With
No. 50 cotton,

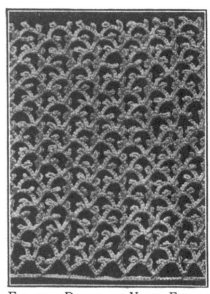

FIG. 21. DETAIL OF YOKE, FIG. 20

make small scallops all around the wings, 2 d s, 4
p 2 d s bet, 2 d s; join at each second p on edge
of wings.

LARGE BUTTERFLY.—Make in the same way. In
the large loop thirty sets 5-5 sts; first side loop
twelve sets; second side loop
ten sets; lower part of wing
twenty sets. Body eleven sets
of 4-4 sts with ps as in Fig.
31. *Antennae*—Make p, then
about an inch of d s, draw
very close to make a firm
curve, pass through head loop,
and sew under body, and the
body sew between the wings.

FERN LEAVES.—Use No. 50
cotton. Begin at small end
of fern; small p, 3 d s, reverse,
3 p 2 d s bet, form a leaf
drawing thread closely, join
p. Reversing 3 d s forms the
curve toward the sts of the
reversed leaf. Work 1 set 2-2

FRONT POINTS OF COLLAR.—Make 4 loops and 4
chains, then a clover leaf with one set of 4-4 sts
between rings. Baste the edging around the collar
very evenly, and sew to the net before making the
last two rows.

First Outer Row—Is all around the collar. At
the neck only, of 4 sets 4-4 sts, join 3d p of r,
and the net too; between rings, 1 d s, p, 1 d s; join
3d p of next r and the net. Continue around the collar
with 5 sets of 4-4 sts, and between rings, 1 set of
3-3 sts, p in centre.

Second Outer Row—This last row omit around the
neck. Join p bet scallops, make 2 sets 4-4 sts, 6 ps
2 d s bet, 2 sets 4-4 sts; join p between scallops.

APPLIQUÉ OF MOTIFS AND COILS.—Place a large
butterfly, a pair of ferns, and three coils, on the
back; a small butterfly, smaller ferns, and three coils
on each shoulder; and a flower motif with cluster of
three coils, on each front. *Coils.* (See Fig. 85.)—Work

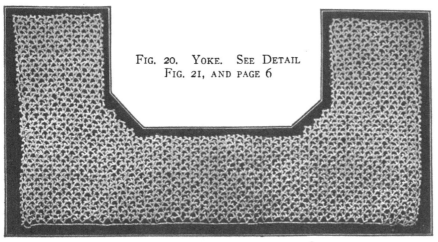

FIG. 20. YOKE. SEE DETAIL
FIG. 21, AND PAGE 6

8

sts for stem, reverse; 4 p 2 d s bet; form second leaf on opposite side of stem by joining shuttle thread to p at beginning of ch. I set 2-2 sts p, repeat last leaf, but after reversing, join 2d p of first leaf, the joining counting as a p. This is the second leaf on the first side of stem, join p at beginning, make stem, and continue. Increase the number of d s by 1 before reversing, and ps by 1 after reversing, but each pair of leaves has the same number of sts. On one side each leaf is joined to the one before on the same side to form the curve. After the third set of leaves increase the stem-stitch to sets of 3-3, toward the end to 4-4. The fern leaves at the back have fifteen pairs of leaves. At the end make one and a half inches of tatted cord, sets of 4-4, sew in a coil as shown in the cut. The ferns on the shoulders have nine pairs of leaves; increase in size by two; and the stems are linked together.

FLOWER ON ENDS OF COLLAR. (See Fig. 32.)—*Top of flower*. Leave a p at beginning, make 12 p 3 d s bet, 9 d s, this forms the scroll before the first upper petal; reverse, 2 d s, join p of scroll, 8 p 2 d s bet, join last p of scroll; reverse, 5 d s, for space between petals, p, 10 d s, join 5th p of first petal; 10 p 2 d s bet, join p of ch. Make three more petals, increasing by one the number of ds and ps. The last ch at end of petals is of 3 d s only. For the other half, begin with the scroll, at 9th p join 9th p of first

FIG. 23. TRIMMING OF METAL THREAD. SEE PAGE 7

FIG. 22. WILD ROSE SPRAY OF BLACK SILK. SEE PAGE 6

scroll, continue as before. *Outside row of tatting ccrds*—Join thread in 1st p of first petal, make a ch of four sets of 4-4 sts, join 1st p of next petal; continue until the fifth petal, then make ten sets and join last ch of 3 d s. *Centre of flower*—Make loop of 5 d s, 26 p 2 d s bet, 5 d s; join by crossing ch, draw closely; make stem with ch of sets of 4-4 sts. Sew all ends of threads left, very closely. *Leaf cluster on stem*—P, 3 d s, p, 10 d s; reverse, 10 p 2 d s bet, join p; loop 5 d s, 15 p 2 d s bet, 4 d s; join, 1 d s, p, 1 d s; make leaf as the other, join after 10 d s to last p made, then 3 d s join p of beginning, 3 d s, then ch of sets of 4-4 sts, and join to long stem. Repeat for the other leaf cluster, a little larger, 12 p on leaves, 21 p on loop.

Figure 27. Medallion.—Centre r, 1 d s, 8 long p 3 d s between (bet), 2 d s. Make eight points thus: R, 3 p 3 d s bet, ch 3 p 5 d s bet, join p of centre r, 3 p 5 d s bet; repeat. Join p at top of point; ch 7 p 3 d s bet; trefoil, side rings 5 p 3 d s bet, centre r 3 d s, join p of side r, 4 d s, 5 p 2 d s bet, 4 d s, p, 3 d s; join the rings of the points and the trefoils.

Figure 28. Flower for Hair.—Use No. 30 crochet cotton and milliner's fine covered wire. Cut wire for each of six petals 6 inches in length. Cover wire closely with double crochet, beginning and ending ½-inch from ends of wire.

TATTED EDGE.—Join threads at beginning of crocheted covering, 5 p separated by 2 d s, join 5th

FIG. 24. DAISY SPRAY OF BLACK SILK. SEE PAGE 7

9

st in crochet from first joining. Continue whole length of wire, bring ends together and fasten.

CENTRE OF PETALS.—With shuttle thread make clover leaf 4 d s, p, 3 d s, 3 p 1 d s between (bet), 3 d s, p, 4 d s, close, make lock-stitch by drawing loop of shuttle thread under connecting thread, pass shuttle through loop, draw close. Leave a little thread between this r and next r. R 4 d s, p, 3 d s, 5 p 1 d s bet, 3 d s, p, 4 d s, close, lock-stitch, join at 1st p of the first ring; repeat first ring.

Leave ¼-inch thread and make r on opposite side from last r made, of 5 d s, join first p, first r of clover leaf, 4 d s, 3 p 1 d s bet, 4 d s, p, 5 d s, close; leaving ¼-inch thread, repeat on the other

Figure 29. Jabot with Battenberg Rings.— Two large Battenberg rings, 2 medium sized and 1 small ring are needed for this jabot, aside from the cotton.

Around one of the medium-sized rings make 10 rings and chains alternating. The ring is of 3 d s, 3 p 3 d s between (bet), 3 d s, and joined to centre by middle p. Chain of 4 d s, 5 ps 4 d s bet, 4 d s. Fasten 2 ch to the second Battenberg ring by middle picots. Fasten the small ring above the last with needle and thread. Around the wheel and 2 rs are rs and chs as in wheel, but ch of 3 ps. Join 6 r to small Battenberg r, 2 each side of the large r and 14 to the wheel.

FIG. 25. COLLAR IN TATTING APPLIQUÉ ON NET. SEE DETAILS FIGS. 26, 30, 31, 32 AND PAGE 7

side, and join. Continue from one side to other until there are five pairs of r besides the clover leaf, each a little smaller than the preceding pair, as the petals grow narrower toward base; fasten in position in wired outer edge with pins, then sew by picots to under side of wire with fine thread. Spread the wire loops so that the inside work will fit tight, that the fagoting between r may be effective.

For centre make large r of 10 p separated by 2 d s, close, surround by small scallops of two threads, 3 d s, 5 p 2 d s bet and 3 d s.

The stamens can be bought. Pass stems of stamens through centre of r last made, arrange petals around centre, wind closely to cover all wire, bend petals to suit taste.

For the upper part sew the 2 largest rs together. To each of them attach 3 clover-leaves, each r of 5 d s, 5 p 3 d s between, 5 d s. Join to ring by first and last picots of first and third rings.

For the crocheted ornament, ch 4 and join. In the ring make 10 doubles (d), then 2 d in each of the 10 d. Make 5 plain rounds, then d in every other d, making 10 d. Stuff with cotton and close by making d in every other d. Fasten two ornaments in the centre and run a knot of black velvet ribbon through the two large rs.

Figure 1, Page 2. Centrepiece. *Materials.—* Five balls No. 20 crochet cotton, and a bolt of coronation cord (see page 14, Fig. 32½). Diameter,

22 inches. Form a r of 10 threads 1⅛-in. in diameter inside, fill it closely with treble crochet, with a second row of double crochet, taking up every st.

1st row—Join centre r, ch 3 d s, 3 p 3 d s between (bet), 3 d s, join 3d st of r, continue around making 16 scallops.

2d row—Join middle (mid) p of ch, ch 3 d s, 3 p 3 d s bet, 3 d s, join mid-p of next ch, repeat.

3d row—Repeat last row with chains 3 d s, 3 p 4 d s bet, 3 d s.

4th row—The same with chains 4 d s, 3 p 4 d s bet, 4 d s.

5th row—With chains 5 d s, 3 p 4 d s bet, 5 d s.

6th row—Join thread and cord to centre p of a scallop, ch 3 d s, 3 p 4 d s bet, 3 d s, make a loop of two sections of cord and join to it, repeat ch, join with next section of cord to mid-p of a scallop, repeat.

7th row—Of sixteen coils of tatting. Wind a yard or two of thread on the shuttle, hold the doubled end firmly, and ch 55 p 3 d s bet. Draw the thread close enough to form a coil as it is made. At 33d p, join the centre p of ch in last row at the left of a loop of cord; at 36th p join centre p of next ch, at 40th p join the next loop of cord, after 55th p, 3 d s and join next cord loop, close and sew in place.

8th row—Join coil at 4th p from joining with a cord loop; ch 3 p 3 d s bet, join 3d p around coil; make three of these scallops on a coil, and join 4th p of next coil.

9th row—Carry thread to p of scallop bet coils, make ch of 2 p 3 d s bet, join mid-p of next scallop; then two ch of 3 p 3 d s bet, joining mid-

FIG. 26. SECTION OF COLLAR, FIG. 25

ps, and one ch of 2 p 3 d s bet, join p of scallop between coils.

10th row—Join p of scallop last made and the first p of next scallop; make three ch of 3 p 4 d s bet; join between coils every 4th ch to ps of two scallops.

11th row—Join ps of two ch; ch 3 d s, 3 p 4 d s bet, 3 d s, join last p of next ch; ch 3 p 4 d s bet, join mid-p of next ch; repeat ch, join 1st p of next ch; ch 3 d s, 3 p 4 d s bet, 3 d s, join ps of chs between coils.

12th row—Join 1st p of 2 ch between coils; ch 3 p 5 d s bet, join mid-p of next ch; repeat twice, joining last as first.

13th row—Of 16 half-wheels, made with shuttle thread alone. R 1 d s, 7 p 3 d s bet, 5 d s; join two ps of chs directly over the joining between coils, 4 d s, close r. Carry thread to next p of scallop, leave ⅛-inch thread; small r 4 d s, join 1st p of r, 4 d s; leave ⅛-inch thread; large r 3 d s, p, 3 d s join 1st p of next scallop, 5 p 3 d s bet. Alternate small and large rs, making seven of each, join large rs together, and the last one to a scallop of the last row.

14th row—Join mid-p of first large r of the half-wheel, ch 3 ps 4 d s bet, join centre p of next large r, continue around half-wheel; bar of 4 d s, join mid-p of first r of next half-wheel.

15th row—Carry thread to mid-ps of last and first scallops in last row; ch 3 p 4 d s bet; join mid-p of next scallop, repeat around half-wheel, join as at first.

16th row—Carry thread to mid-p, first ch of last row, join; ch 5 d s, 3 p 4 d s bet, 5 d s; repeat

FIG. 27. MEDALLION. SEE PAGE 9

last row and add bar of 4 d s bet wheels.

17th row—Join thread and cord to mid-p of first scallop; ch 3 p 4 d s bet, join next section of cord; repeat ch, join with cord, mid-p of next scallop; repeat ch, join cord with a loop of two sections, shuttle thread over, ball thread under the crossing, 1 d s, repeat with two more loops, repeat ch, join with cord mid-p of next scallop, repeat ch and join cord, repeat ch and with cord join mid-p of next scallop, repeat ch and with cord join first scallop of next wheel.

18th row—Consists of sixteen wheels. Centre coil made as before, sew the ends fast. Join p of coil, ch 6 d s, 5 p 3 d s bet, 3 d s; coil this ch back upon itself and join, shuttle thread over, ball thread under, at centre of 6 d s, and draw tightly; 3 d s, join next p but one of coil. Make thirteen r around coil. Join mid-p of a r in last row; ch 2 d s, 5 p 3 d s bet, 2 d s; join mid-p of next r, continue around wheel. Carry thread to ps of two adjoining r of last row. Repeat ch with 6 p and join 2 p between scallops. Join last 5 scallops to the main work thus: 4th p of ch to outside loop of cord; 4th p of next ch to 3d p of next ch but one; 2d p of next ch to 1st p of ch on main work, also 6th p same ch to last p of next ch but one on

main work, and add a 7th p to this ch; 2d p of next ch to 1st p next ch on main work; 3d p of next ch to cord loop. The wheels may be sewed on if preferred.

19th row—R 9 ps 3 d s bet; join 2d p to mid-p of free scallop nearest the cord loop, 5th p to centre cord loop, and 8th p to mid-p first scallop on next wheel. Ch, 3 p 3 d s bet, join 2 p between scallops, continue around with 7 p to each ch, joining wheels by the r. Press carefully, on flannel, right side down; cover with a damp cloth and use a hot iron.

Figure 33. Doily. *Materials.*—Crochet cotton No. 20 and coronation cord (see page 14, Fig. 32½). Make a r one-inch in diameter inside, by winding thread eight times, and fill closely with double crochet. Make the cross inside the ring, by sewing three threads across each way, and covering with over and under stitches. *1st row*—Join thread to r, and fill the space with 18 scallops, ch 5 d s, p, 5 d s joined to the r.

2d row—Join thread, or carry it to a p on ch, ch 6 d s, p, 6 d s, join p on next scallop; continue around.

3d row—Carry thread to a p, join cord to a p of the r, ch 4 d s, 3 p 3 d s between (bet), 3 d s; make loop of

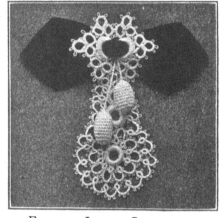

FIG. 29. JABOT. SEE PAGE 10

two sections of cord, join ch; make ch 3 d s, 3 p 3 d s bet, 4 d s; join next cord section, and the p next but one to the last joining.

4th row—Clover leaf of three r, 3 d s, 7 p 2 d s bet, 3 d s; join by 1st p together, and the centre r by two upper ps to 2 chs of last row, as shown in the cut. Ch 7 p 3 d s bet, join loop of cord; repeat ch then repeat clover leaf.

5th row—Join 2d p in ch; ch 4 d s, p, 4 d s, join next p but one. Repeat around.

6th row—Ch 3 d s, 3 p 3 d s bet, 3 d s; join ps of last row, except those over clover leaves and joinings.

7th and 8th rows—Chains of 4 d s, 3 p 4 d s bet, 4 d s, and joined in every ch of last rows.

9th row—Join thread and cord to p at top of scallop, ch 3 d s, 3 p 3 d s bet, 3 d s, join with next section of cord, to mid-p of next scallop, ch 3 d s, 3 p 3 d s bet, 2 d s, make two loops of cord, and join to them only; ch 2 d s, 3 p 3 d s bet, 3 d s; with cord join mid-p of next scallop last row. Repeat around.

10th row—Make clover leaf, 3 d s, 6 p 2 d s bet, 3 d s; join rs together and centre r by mid-p to ch of the last row. Ch 5 p, 2 d s bet, join first loop of cord, repeat ch, join second loop of cord, repeat ch, then repeat clover leaf. Continue around.

11th row—R 2 d s, p, 2 d s, join first and last ps of 2 ch of the row before, 2 d s, p, 2 d s; ch 3 d s, 3 p

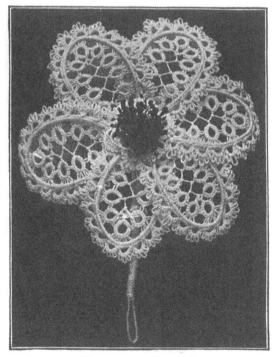

FIG. 28. FLOWER FOR HAIR. SEE PAGE 9

12

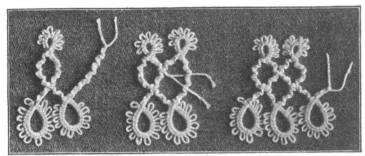

FIG. 30. LATTICE WORK FOR COLLAR, FIG. 25

2 d s bet, 3 d s; repeat r and join centre of clover leaf, as last r; ch 3 d s, 3 p 2 d s bet, 3 d s, repeat r and join; over the ch between the loops of cord, repeat the ch, but with 5 p.

Figure 34. Doily. (See detail of cord, page 14, Fig. 32½.)—The centre, including the trefoil row, is made like the large doily in Fig. 33, with these exceptions: The centre is smaller in diameter, inside; has two threads only in the cross; and but one row of chs around the first row; and but six clover leaves. *4th row*—Join thread to a p each of two ch outside of the clover leaf; ch 3 d s, 3 p 3 d s bet, 3 d s, join 3d p in ch, repeat ch, joining every other p in last row and 2 p between chs and leaves. *5th row*—R 2 d s p, 2 d s, join first and last p of 2 chs of the row before, 2 d s, p, 2 d s; ch 3 d s, 3 p 3 d s bet, 3 d s; repeat r; repeat ch; repeat r; ch of 5 p, which repeat every 3d ch.

FIG. 31. BODY OF BUTTERFLY. SEE FIGS. 25, 26

Figure 35. Table Scarf. —Four balls of crochet cotton No. 20 are used.

LARGE MEDALLION. *Square in the central motif* (see Fig. 39)—R 3 d s, 3 p 2 d s between (bet), 3 d s; ch 5 d s, p, 3 d s; turn, r 5 d s, join last p of r, 5 d s; ch 3 d s, p, 3 d s, p, 3 d s; r 5 d s, join mid-p 1st r, 5 d s; ch 3 d s, p, 5 d s, join last p of 1st r; ch 5 d s, p, 5 d s, join base of 1st r; ch 5 d s, p, 5 d s, join p in 1st ch; ch 3 p 2 d s bet, join p of next ch; ch 5 p 2 d s bet, join next p, same ch; ch 3 p 2 d s bet, join next p; ch 5 d s, p, 5 d s, join bet next 2 chs. Leave ⅙th of an inch of thread, and repeat from the beginning 3 times.

BORDER AROUND THE SQUARE. — Begin at the outer end. * R, 2 p 7 d s bet; repeat the r and draw closely; ch 2 p 7 d s bet, join 2d p of 2d r; repeat ch; repeat r, join 1st p to the joining of ch and the last r; repeat r closely, join opposite r; repeat ch; repeat r, join with 1st p, the last r; repeat r closely; turn, repeat ch in the opposite direction from the last, join 2d p to mid-p of scallop at right of a corner of the square, and join at end of the ch the 2d p of last r, leaving its 1st r free inside of the ch; repeat ch, join 1st p to 2d p of corner scallop of the square; repeat r, join 2d p to joining of ch and last r; repeat

r closely; turn and repeat ch in opposite direction from the last, join 1st p to opposite ch; * repeat r, join 1st p to last r. Beginning with this last r (which repeats the first) repeat from * 7 times, join square and form a circle around it, close.

EDGING AROUND CENTRE MEDALLION.—Join upper p at right side of a point; ch 3 p 3 d s bet; r 3 p 4 d s bet; repeat ch; ring; then 3 ch crossing the top of next point; repeat around.

SMALL MEDALLION (see Fig. 40).—The two medallions finish the ends of the insertion. Centre r, 8 p 2 d s bet; ch 3 d s, join p of ring, make a very small p; repeat around, close. * R, 3 d s, join p of centre r, 3 d s; turn, r, 5 d s, p, 5 d s; turn, ch 7 d s, p, 7 d s; r 5 d s, join p of last r 5 d s; ch 7 d s, p, 7 d s, join between the first two r; ch 3 d s; repeat small r joining centre r; turn, ch 7 d s, p, 7 d s; r 3 d s, p, 3 d s, join p of first ch; 3 d s, p, 3 d s; ch 3 d s, 3 p 2 d s bet, 3 d s; r 3 p 3 d s bet; ch 7 d s, join p of last ch, 7 d s. * Repeat between stars three times. *Row around medallion*—of chs 3 p 3 d s bet, joining ps of rs, mid-ps of chs, and top of the pair of r.

In this piece of work, but especially in the small medallion, it is very important that chs and rs should be turned in the right direction in making.

WIDE BORDER. — Make a square motif like the centre of the large medallion; below it a three-quarter square, joined to it, in making, by the ps. *The oval*

FIG. 32. MOTIF IN COLLAR, FIG. 25

motif next; centre r 10 p 2 d s bet. R 3 d s, p, 8 d s, p, 8 d s, p, 3 d s; join p of centre; r 3 d s, join last r, 6 d s, p, 6 d s, p 3 d s, join centre r; repeat last r three times, then one like the 1st r, and four like the 2d r. Edge the oval with a row of chs of 3 p 3 d s bet, joined to ps of the oval, and to the motifs on each side. *Edging on ends and around the border,* of chs of 3 p 2 d s bet.

NARROW BORDER. — R 3 p 2 d s bet, 6 d s; ch 3

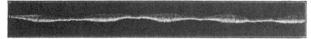

FIG. 32½. CORONATION CORD, FULL SIZE, USED IN CENTREPIECE FIG. 1, AND DOILIES FIGS. 33 AND 34

d s, p, 3 d s, join 1st p; repeat ch, join next p; repeat again, join last p; turn, ch 4 d s, p, 4 d s; make one-quarter of a square motif; and alternate the figures across the end. *To finish.* — Baste the insertion to the linen, 6 inches from the end. With two strands of embroidery floss buttonhole-stitch closely around the insertion, catching every p of the tatting. Button-hole the edgings on in the same way. Press and cut away the cloth.

Figure 36. Collar. (See detail, Fig. 37.) — Use crochet cotton No. 40 on the shuttle, No. 60 on the ball. For fuller explanation of lattice-work, see page 7.

LATTICE-WORK. (See Fig. 37.) — Work p, 1 d s, p; 4 sets 4-4 sts; ch 4 d s, 7 p 2 d s between (bet), 3 d s.

FIG. 34. DOILY. SEE FIGS. 1 AND 33, AND PAGE 13

Draw the ch close to the sets of sts, and form the first small loop of the neck, by crossing the ch at its beginning, shuttle thread over, ball thread under the ch. Make the lattice ch of 9 sets 4-4 sts, join p left at beginning, drawing the ball thread back firmly. Draw the ball thread between the lattice, and work 2 sets 4-4 sts; draw the ball thread back, which leaves shuttle thread above, ball thread under the work. Cross the long lattice ch 2 sets below the loop for the neck. Work 2 sets 4-4 sts and a loop of 7 ps, as the first. Work another lattice ch of 9 sets 4-4 sts, join the first lattice ch of 9 sets, two sets from the last crossing, leaving the threads on opposite sides of the work; work 2 sets 4-4 sts, and cross the lattice ch as before. Always in joining over the lattice ch draw the shuttle thread tight, so that the ball thread is double around the ch, and the shuttle thread straight through the joining. Continue until there are 60 of the 7-p loops for the neck of the collar.

2d row — Work 5 sets 4-4 sts, join the last lattice ch two sets from the last joining. Continue around the lattice edge, joining each 5 sets 4-4 sts to the centre of a lattice scallop of the last row, and keeping the work the same side up.

3d row — At the end of the collar carry threads to centre of last scallop of last row, and work back as the row before, but join with the shuttle thread.

4th row — Divide the lattice-work into 5 parts of 10 scallops at each end, 11 scallops to the 3, in order to leave one scallop between the points. Work each

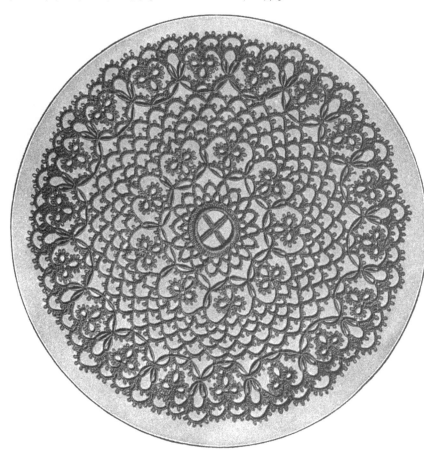

FIG. 33. DOILY. SEE FIGS. 1 AND 34, AND PAGE 12

to a point, working back and forth as before; carrying threads to centre of last scallop, to leave one less on each row. Cut and sew threads at finish of each point.

1st row around points—With neck held toward the worker, join centre of first lattice square at the right; work 2 d s, 7 p 2 d s bet; reverse, ch 6 d s; draw shuttle thread closely, and join the next lattice square, 6 d s; reverse, ch 2 d s, 7 p 2 d s bet, 2 d s, reverse,

the last row. Join lattice squares as at the right side.

AROUND THE NECK.—Work 5 sets 4-4 sts, join 2d p of first small loop at the neck; work 5 sets 4-4 sts, join 2d p, opposite side of same loop, 1 d s, join 2d p of next loop; continue around neck. The points being finished, baste the lattice-work on the pattern right side down, firmly at the neck, leaving the other edge free, press the points out smoothly. On the pattern it will keep the shape better while joining

FIG. 35. TABLE SCARF. SEE DETAILS FIGS. 39, 40, AND PAGE 13

6 d s, join. Repeat around the 5 points, with an added scallop and two joinings at points, and skipping the extra square between points.

2d row around points—Join last ch of 7 p to last lattice square; carry threads to centre p of ch last made, work back around points with chs of 4 sets 4-4 sts, with a p in centre, and join at centre ps of last rows. Continue around the points, with an added ch at each point, and skipping the scallops between points, as in

the other parts, and avoid soiling. For the rest of the collar use only No. 60 cotton.

MOTIF BETWEEN THE FRONT POINTS. (See Fig. 37.) —The clover leaf (c l) is made of a small p and 13 sets 4-4 sts, form loop crossing 1 d s from beginning. Ch 15 sets 4-4 sts, cross one set from first loop; repeat first loop, and work 3 sets for stem. Ch 3 d s, p, 1 d s, reverse; 3 d s, 12 p 2 d s bet, reverse; 12 d s, join by ball thread to p after first 3 d s. This makes the first reversed petal. Work 5 d s, p, 1 d s, reverse and proceed with second petal. Join the 4th p to last p of petal before. Join between 4th and 5th petals to the c l. After three more petals, ch 3 d s, join centre petal of c l, 3 d s, and continue with the seven petals reversed, as shown in Fig. 37. Join the first reversed petal at the top to the petal before. After last petal, ch 3 d s and join stem of c l.

Row around the motif— This joins to points on the collar. Work 12 sets 4-4 sts, join 2 ch between points of the collar, by ball thread. Work 12 sets more, join where this ch began. Work 7 sets, join 2d ch from last joining, 4 sets, join 11th p on first petal and 5th p on second petal together. Work 4 sets, join second scallop from last joining, 3 sets and join next two petals. Continue around motif with scallops of 7 sets, and join collar as on the first side.

MOTIF BETWEEN THE BACK POINTS.—Work p, 6 d s, p, 10 d s, reverse; 2 d s, 10 p 2 d s bet, join 1st p; making the first petal. Reverse, 6 d s, p 12 d s, reverse; 12 p 2 d s between, join p, making the second petal. Make a third petal with 14 plain d s and 14 p. Work 6 d s, p, 4 d s, then 25 p, 3 d s; form a long loop, crossing ch just past the single p. Make the large loop of 12 d s, 35 p, 4 d s; cross ch 4 d s before 1st p. The other long loop repeats the first, reversed. Make three petals as the first three, reversed. After last petal make 6 d s, join p at beginning.

Row around motif—Work 9 sets 4-4 sts, join; (on the inside of the motif) to p at close of the first long side loop; 3 sets, join p at close of third long loop, 9 sets, join at starting-point. Work 8 sets, join collar between points, 8 sets, join at starting-point. Work 8 sets, join collar at second scallop from last joining; 3 sets, join first and second petals. Continue around motif with chs long enough to clear the ps. Make one joining

FIG. 36½. DETAIL OF DOILY FIG. 38

on the long side loop, and two on the long centre loop.

FERNS ON THE POINTS.—Work p, 3 d s, 3 p 2 d s bet, 3 d s, join p at beginning; 1 d s, p, 5 d s, reverse; 2 d s, 5 p, 2 d s, form leaf by joining p at beginning. Work 2 d s, p, 6 d s, reverse; 2 d s, 6 p, 2 d s, form leaf as before, but on opposite side from the first one. Each pair of leaves increases 1 d s and 1 p each. Continue until there are five leaves on one side, six on the other, not counting the small loop at the beginning. As this is a double fern to fit around a front point, the other part is reversed, with 4 d s, p, between. Begin with 15 p, then 15 d s. Make two pairs of each size each time before decreasing the number of sts. After joining each leaf at its base, reverse, 3 d s, p, reverse again, to bring the p on the right side to join the leaf ch. There should be 11 leaves on the outside, and 10 on the inside. Carry threads to the first p of the first outside leaf, and work back around the outside of the two ferns with chs of 4 sets 4-4 sts, joining two leaves together. Continue, increasing the number of sets when needed, leaving a p at centre of each ch, and joining two leaves each time. At the end of the small fern join the flower motif between points of the collar at the first free scallop, after 3 sets 4-4 sts; 3 more sets, join first free scallop on lattice point; 3 sets, join first leaf on fern. Continue across ferns, joining two leaves together, as on the outside. At the neck continue with three lattice scallops to the point, Turn, work back in the same way to the fern, making the last scallop around the small end loop. Cut and sew ends. Care must be taken to have the ferns made in pairs to fit. The lattice-work has right

FIG. 36. COLLAR. SEE DETAIL FIG. 37, AND PAGE 14

16

FIG. 37. DETAIL OF COLLAR FIG. 36

according to judgment, joining the centre of each lattice scallop. The second, of the lattice scallops, made large enough to give a graceful finish to the edge, and joined to ps of adjoining scallops of the row before.

Figure 38. Doily. (See Detail Fig. 36½.)—Use No. 16 spool cotton or No. 30 crochet cotton.

1st row—R 3 p 4 d s between (bet), ch 2 p 4 d s bet; make 12 of each with the rs joined together; join the 20 circles by ps of adjoining chs; 2 p the inner joining, 1 p the outer joining. Baste the work on stiff paper and make the spider-web as in drawn-work.

2d row—Clover leaf (c l), r 4 d s, join 1st p of second ch, left side of the 1 p joining, 4 d s; centre r, 4 d s, join p of next ch, 4 d s, join p of opposite ch; repeat first r, join next p; ch 4 d s; r 4 d s, join, 4 d s; ch 4 d s, p, 4 d s. Make 6 r and 5 ch in all; repeat ch 4 d s, and c l.

3d row—Join c l, ch 2 p 4 d s bet, join p; repeat around scallop, after c l join 1st p to ch before.

Inside row—C l, 8 d s, join 1st p, 2d ch before joining, 9 d s; centre r 6 d s, join 2d p, 5 d s, join opposite p, 6 d s; repeat first r, joining 2d p; ch 3 p 4 d s bet; r 4 d s, join next p; ch 4 d s, p, 4 d s, repeat r, join, repeat first ch. Repeat around. Roll the edge of the linen, buttonhole-stitch around, catching in the ps of the tatting.

Figure 41. Bonbon Basket.—No. 15 crochet cotton is used.

Make r of 5 p 3 d s between (bet), close tightly, and tie threads to make a 6th p. Ch 2 d s, p, 2 d s, join 1st p. Repeat, making 6 ch. *2d row*—3 d s, p, 3 d s; repeat around. *3d row*—4 d s, p, 4 d s; repeat.

and wrong sides, and the work must be kept right side up in all parts. Therefore, begin at the end of the long fern for the opposite side, and reverse the directions.

Ferns at Shoulder Points.—They are made and joined as those described of six leaves on the inside, and seven on the outside, for the front one; and seven on each side of the one at the back of the second point. These ferns are connected by a coil made of five rows of ch — plain d s — the last, of ps 3 d s bet (see Fig. 85). Work around the coils a row of lattice scallops of 2 sets 4-4 sts, p, 2 sets. Join twice on each side to the ends of the ferns.

Ferns at the Back.—Made as the others, with 9 leaves on the inside, and 10 on the outside. The size of leaves is not increased after 20 d s and 20 p. A cluster of three coils joins the ferns, the upper ones oval; join them and work lattice scallops around the cluster, joining the ferns and point of the collar. Add a c l at each side, joined twice each; to the ferns, the coils, and lattice chs of the collar.

Edging Around the Collar.—With the exception of the neck, work 2 rows around the collar. The first, scallops of ps, varying

FIG. 38. DOILY. SEE FIG. 36½, AND PAGE 17

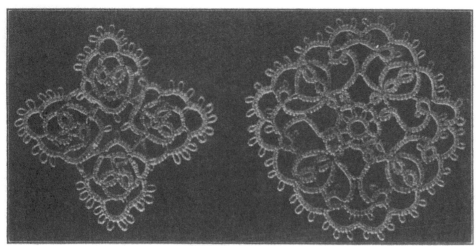

FIG. 39. DETAIL OF SCARF FIG. 35   FIG. 40. DETAIL OF SCARF FIG. 35

Figure 43. Frog for
Coat.—Use white crochet
silk. Make coils with continuous thread, in the tat-
ting-cord effect. See "Sets
of Stitches" on page 3.
ROUND COIL. — One p,
ch 12 d s, join p, form-
ing a close r. Work a
row of d s and sew it
around the r. The next
four rows are of sets of
4-4 sts, each row sewed
to position as made.
Draw shuttle-thread very
tight to give the crimped
appearance to the ch.
The last row of d s, ps
3 d s between (bet).

4th row—5 d s, p, 5 d s. This forms the bottom of
the basket. STAND OF THE BASKET. — R 3 p 4 d s
bet; ch 5 d s, r 3 d s, join last p, 4 d s, p, 3 d s;
ch 5 d s, join last row. Repeat large and small rs
and chs around, joining the bottom. UPPER PART.—
R 3 p, 4 d s bet; ch 5 d s; r 3 d s, join last p, 2 d s,
p, 2 d s, p, 3 d s; ch 5 d s, join p of third circle of
the bottom; repeat around. SIDES. — R 3 p 2 d s bet,
join 2d p to p of last row; ch 4 d s; r 4 d s, 5 p
3 d s bet, 4 d s; ch 4 d s; r 3 p 4 d s bet, join 1st p
to first r, and 2d p to bottom; ch 4 d s; r 4 d s,
join second r, 4 p 3 d s bet, 4 d s; repeat around.
RIM.— R 5 p 3 d s bet, join 3d p of a r in last row;
ch 3 d s, join last p of last r, 3 d s, p, 2 d s, p, 2 d s, p, 3
d s, p, 3 d s, join 3d p of next ring, last row; r, 5 p 3 d s
bet, join 1st p to last p of ch; repeat around.
HANDLE.—Ch 13 p 6 d s between, fasten to opposite
side of basket, ch back joining each p with 6 d s
between. If the basket is made very firmly, it will
not need stiffening, but directions for stiffening are
as follows: One cup of sugar and one-half cup of
water are boiled to form a syrup, but not until it
threads. The basket is immersed in this while it is
hot, the surplus syrup squeezed out, and it is ready
to shape. It is very easy to color these baskets any
desired shade by stirring into the liquid the necessary
amount of fruit coloring. A few drops of red ink
makes a
beautiful pink,
while coffee
used instead
of water gives
a variety of
brown shades,
from cream to
a deep brown,
according to
the strength
of the coffee
used. One can
experiment
with tea to
obtain a still
different
variety of
shades and
tints.

BUTTON LOOP.—Add a third thread to make this. Ball
thread and third thread pass around the hand alike,
keep the thread separated on the fingers, and do not
cross them in using. With the third thread make
1 d s, reverse by dropping that thread from three
fingers, retaining it between the thumb and finger; with
the ball thread make 1 d s; reverse and make 1 d s

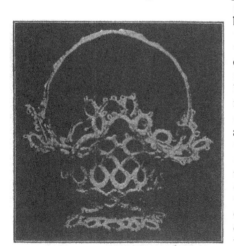

FIG. 41. BONBON BASKET. SEE PAGE
17

FIG. 42. DETAIL OF DOILY FIG. 44

with the third thread. Continue until there is the length required. OVAL COILS.—One p, 10 sets of 4-4 sts, p; 12 sets of 4-4 sts; loop the 12 sets crossing the ch after the last p; shuttle thread over, ball thread under the ch. Make 10 sets 4-4 sts, join p at beginning. Make two rows around the oval, joining the ps at top and beginning. Sew to under side of work. SCROLL

FIG. 43. FROG FOR COAT. SEE PAGE 18

SECTION.—One p, 30 d s; reverse, 15 p 3 d s bet, join p at beginning. Repeat for opposite scroll. Join in the centre, make another pair of scrolls, of 35 d s, 17 p. Draw the shuttle-thread tightly around centre of both pairs, and close firmly. For the centre scroll, make a ch of one p 16 sets 4-4 sts, loop it by crossing at the beginning. Ch 6 d s, 24 p 2 d s bet, 6 d s. Loop this ch by crossing at the beginning. Ch 6 d s, 24 p 2 d s bet, 6 d s. Loop around last loop and join. For the cord through centre, 8 sets 4-4 sts. Sew to centre. Pass the first pair of scroll leaves through the oval coils; the second pair over the ovals and sew to them. BUTTONS.—Cover button molds with two thicknesses of white silk. One p, 12 d s, join p. Make a row of 4-4 sts, and sew to position. A row of sets of 4-4 sts, with p after each set, and sew on. Join 1st p, 3 d s, p, 3 d s, join next p, continue, there should be 10 small scallops. Join p, make 2 sets 4-4 sts, p. Two sets more, join next scallop, repeat around. Fasten ends neatly, and sew motif to covered mold under the end.

Figure 44. Doily. (See Detail Fig. 42.)—*Materials.*—One ball of No. 40 crochet cotton, and linen four and one-quarter inches in diameter. Turn a narrow edge and finish with button-

hole or feather-stitch. The lattice border is made with continuous thread between shuttle and ball. To leave a picot at the beginning,—tie a single knot in thread between shuttle and ball; take knot between left thumb and finger, pass ball thread around the hand as usual, and (while beginning) pass shuttle thread around left little finger, and back between thumb and finger, holding those fingers together. Work 4 d s, leaving a small p between the knot and first d s, drop thread from little finger, and draw shuttle thread closely. This forms a neat p to begin with, avoids ends and is useful in making even, firm coils. In the "Tatted Cord" effect, a term, as 6 sets of 4-4 sts, would mean, work 4 single sts like the first half of a d s, then 4 single sts like the last half of a d s, six times. To join these cords, draw the ball thread under the ch, pass shuttle through the loop, draw threads so closely, that the ball thread is drawn double around the ch, and the shuttle thread is straight through the joining.

LATTICE BORDER.—Leave a p at beginning, 4 d s, 11 p 2 d s between, 3 d s. Form large loop by crossing this ch 1 d s from beginning. Work very closely to the loop, 6 sets of 4-4 sts; ch 2 d s, 8 small ps, 1 d s between (bet), 2 d s. Form a small loop, crossing at beginning of ch and joining as directed. Work 4 sets of 4-4 sts, cross ch of 6 sets at point 2 sets from the large loop. Work 2 sets of 4-4 sts and make second large loop as the first. Work

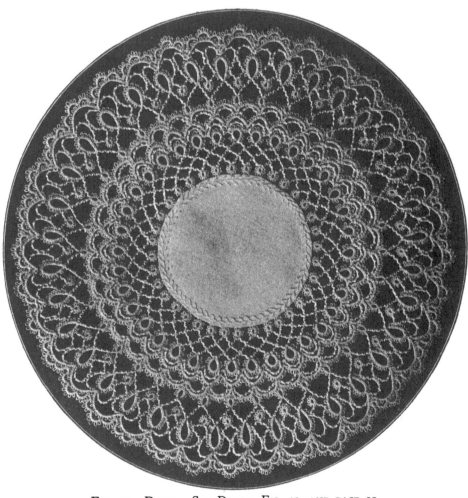

FIG. 44. DOILY. SEE DETAIL FIG. 42, AND PAGE 19

6 sets of 4-4 sts, then a second small loop; 2 sets of 4-4 sts; join first ch of 6 sets at point 2 sets from first small loop. Draw enough of the ball thread through to the shuttle thread to pass it around the hand, and work 2 sets of 4-4 sts. Return the ball thread, bringing the threads on opposite sides of the work. Cross last ch of 6 sets, shuttle thread over, ball thread under the ch, at 2 sets from last large loop. Work 2 sets 4-4 sts, then next large l o o p. Make thirty-six each of large and small loops. To join the ends. When working last ch of 6 sets, join, after 4th set, the first ch made, 2 sets from the first small loop; continue with 2 more sets, and the small loop, then 2 sets joining as usual, again 2 sets, cross last ch, again 2 sets, and join p at beginning of first loop made. To sew to linen centre; baste linen on paper wrong side up, fit the lattice-work evenly around centre on the paper, also wrong side up and sew ps of small loops to edge of linen; then press the work.

First row after Lattice-work.—Join 3d p of a large loop. Work 5 sets of 4-4 sts, draw shuttle thread tight through sts, join 3d p on opposite side of same loop. Work 1 d s, p, 1 d s, join to 3d p of next loop, repeat all around doily.

2d row—Carry threads to p between scallops of last row. Work 3 d s, 9 p 2 d s bet, 3 d s, join to p between next scallops. Repeat.

3d row—Carry threads to centre p of scallops of last row, work 5 sets 4-4 sts, join to centre p of next scallop. Repeat.

4th row—Work 3 d s, 9 p 2 d s bet, 3 d s, joining to next scallop at same place as last row. Repeat. Cut and sew threads.

5th row—With shuttle thread make r of 2 d s, 3 p 2 d s bet, 2 d s, join 2 ps between scallops of last row; repeat first half of r. Join ball thread, work 4 sets 4-4 sts, ch 4 d s, 17 p 2 d s bet, 3 d s; form loop by crossing ch at first d s. Work 4 sets of 4-4 sts, repeat small r, joining between next two scallops. Repeat around; cut threads.

6th r o w—Join 3d p on left of large loop of last row. Work 7 sets of 4-4 sts, join by shuttle thread to 9th p at top of same loop; 5 sets 4-4 sts, p, then 2 sets and join by shuttle t h r e a d

FIG. 45. PANSY IN COLORS. SEE DETAILS FIG. 46, AND PAGE 20

to 3d p on opposite side of same loop. Work 2 sets of 4-4 sts, ch 2 d s, 8 small ps 1 d s bet, 2 d s, form small loop by crossing ch at first d s; 2 sets 4-4 sts, join by shuttle thread to 3d p of next large loop; 2 sets of 4-4 sts, join by ball thread to p left on ch 7 sets between 5th and 6th sets; 5 sets of 4-4 sts, and join at top of loop as before. Repeat around.

7th row—Join at top of large loop over the joining of last row. Work 3 d s, 13 p 2 d s bet, 3 d s, join at top of next large loop; repeat around.

8th row—Carry both threads to 2d p of scallop of last row. Work 3 d s, 3 p 2 d s bet, 3 d s, join 3d p from last joining; 2 d s, 5 p 2 d s bet, 2 d s, join 4th from last joining; 3 d s, 3 p 2 d s bet, 3 d s, join 3d p from last joining which makes 3 small scallops around large scallop. Work one set 3-3 sts, join 2d p on next large scallop. Repeat around.

Figure 45. Pansy. (See Detail Fig. 46.)—Use crochet silk in purple and lavender, cream for edge and yellow for centre.

Wind a very little yellow on the shuttle, and make r of 5 p 3 d s between (bet). *Small Petal*—Wind shuttle with dark purple, without cutting thread join to a p, and ch 13 p 2 d s between, join into same p, ch 11 p 2 d s bet, join into centre p of first ch. Ch 11 p, join into same p in the r.

Middle Petal—Join thread into the next p of r. Ch 15 p 2 d s bet, join into p in r. Ch 13 p, join into centre p of previous ch. Ch 13 p, join into p in r.

Large Petal—Carry threads to next p in r; ch 17 p 2 d s bet, join in same p. Ch 15 p 2 d s bet, join in centre p of previous ch. Ch 15 p, join in same p in centre r. Carry threads to next p in r. Repeat large petal, then the middle petal. Tie and cut threads. Wind shuttle with lavender, join into p at starting point.

SMALL PETAL. —Ch 3 p 2 d s bet, join 3d p of the ch. Make 8 small scallops a r o u n d the petal. C a r r y thread to next petal, and make 10 scallops; on the large petal make 12 scallops. The two large p e t a l s have 2 rows of s c a l l o p s, the

FIG. 46. DETAILS OF PANSY FIG. 45

20

second of 13 scallops, with but 2 p in first and last scallops. Wind shuttle with cream, and work around each petal; first and last scallops of 6 d s, the others 11 d s. Do not press the work, but arrange with the fingers. Overlap the petals as shown in Fig. 45. In fastening on the goods to decorate, tack lightly so as not to flatten the work, as the effect is much more natural if left loose. Different markings may be used to suit taste. Make the stems with silk as near the natural color as possible. Ch d s to make desired length, and tie to the pansy on the wrong side.

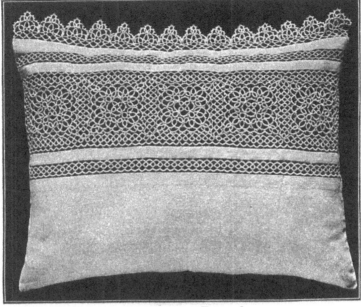

FIG. 47. PILLOW. SEE DETAILS FIGS. 48, 49, AND PAGE 21

Figure 47. Pillow.—For this pillow four balls of crochet cotton are used, No. 5 or as fine as No. 30. To avoid joining, it is an aid to measure the lengths of thread for the shuttle. Coarser numbers require more; for instance, No. 3 requires two-fifths more than No. 30. Of No. 5 for one square; row 1, 2½ yds; row 2, 7 yds; row 3, 2½ yds. For the edging one scallop; middle row 2 yds, upper row ½-yd, lower row ¼-yd.

FIG. 48. DETAIL OF PILLOW FIG. 47

SQUARE. (See Fig. 48.)—Begin with a centre r, a larger r for the daisy centre, repeat thrice, and join in a circle. Then the daisy row all around, then row 3 all around.

1st row—R, 7 d s, small p, 5 d s, p, 5 d s; larger r 5 d s, 5 p 3 d s between (bet), 5 d s, ch 3 p 4 d s bet; repeat small r joining the 1st by the small p; repeat large r; repeat ch. Repeat once, joining small rs.

2d row—* R 9 d s, join 1st p of large r, 3 d s, p, 6 d s; ch 3 p 3 d s bet; r 8 d s, join last r, 3 d s, join centre r, 3 d s, p, 8 d s; ch 3 d s, 2 p 3 d s bet, 6 d s; r 10 d s, join last r, 3 d s, join centre r, 3 d s p 10 d s; ch 6 d s, p 3 d s p 3 d s; r 8 d s join, 3 d s join, 3 d s p 8 d s; ch 3 p 3 d s bet; r 6 d s join, 3 d s join, 9 d s. * Repeat from * to * three times, forming a square of four daisies.

3d row—Join thread to mid-p of last ch at left of a daisy; * ch 3 d s, 3 p 2 d s bet, join 2d p of next ch; ch 3 d s, 2 p 2 d s bet, 3 d s; r

7 d s, join centre r of daisy, 7 d s; ch 3 d s, 4 p 2 d s bet, 3 d s; repeat r, join same place, ch 3 d s, 2 p 2 d s bet, 3 d s, join next p; ch 3 d s, 3 p 2 d s bet, 3 d s, join mid-p of next ch; ch 4 d s, 3 p 2 d s bet, 4 d s, join mid-p first ch of next daisy *. Repeat from * to * thrice.

INSERTION.—Around and joining squares. R 4 d s, 3 p 4 d s bet, 4 d s; ch 4 d s p 4 d s; join the rs. Border the first square with this, the first row of the insertion, joining it by the chs to every second p of the square, except at the corners. The two corner chs and half chs on each side of them, of 5 d s instead of 4 d s, and two r joined with no ch between. The two corner chs of the insertion join to mid-ps of the corner ch of the square. Border three sides of the second square, and join to the first by the chs. At the corner join the 3d p of r to the joining of 2 corner r, ch 5 d s join 3d p of corner ch 5 d s, skip one insertion r and join next r; join every 2d p of the square by the centre of chs. Having joined the 5 squares, border all around with the second insertion row of chs, 4 d s p 4 d s,—adding a r where needed at the corners. The two insertion bands of the pillow are of the same pattern as that around the squares.

EDGING. (See Fig. 49.)—Begin with the middle row. * R 6 d s, 3 p 3 d s bet, 6 d s; ch 5 d s, 3 p 3 d s bet, 3 d s; r 8 d s, join 1st r, 2 p 3 bet, 8 d s; ch, 3 p 3 d s bet, r 10 d s, join last r, 2 p 3 d s bet, 10 d s; ch 3 p 3 d s bet; r 8 d s join, 2 p 3 d s bet, 8 d s; ch 3 d s, 3 p 3 d s bet, 5 d s; r 6 d s, join, 2 p 3 d s bet 6 d s *. Repeat from * to *, and join the first ch, of next daisy, after 5 d s, to the last p of the last ch.

Lower row—Having made the last ch of the middle row, turn; * ch 6 d s p 6 d s; join p of last r; ch 6 d s p 6 d s; r 5 d s, join the last r of the middle row, 3 d s join next r; continue joining with

FIG. 49. DETAIL OF PILLOW FIG. 47

3 d s bet around the daisy, 5 d s; ch 6 d s p 6 d s, join next p. * Repeat from * to *.

Upper row—Join thread on mid-p of the 1st daisy ch. * Ch 5 d s, 3 p 3 d s bet, 3 d s; join mid-p of next ch; ch 3 d s, 2 p 3 d s bet, 3 d s; r 7 d s, join centre r of daisy, 7 d s; ch 3 p 3 d s bet; repeat r, join in same place; ch 2 p 3 d s bet, join mid-p of next ch; ch 3 d s, 3 p 3 d s bet, 5 d s, join the two p of the chs below; join chs at the first p after 5 d s. * Repeat between stars. The edging is rounded for a fluted edge, but may be straightened

FIG. 50. DOILY. SEE PAGE 22

by enlarging the centre rs of the daisies. This work needs to be kept very even and closely drawn up, and some of the ps should be very small, to join compactly.

Figure 50. Doily.—*1st row*—R, 9 p 2 d s between (bet), with ball and shuttle, make a circle, r, 4 d

FIG. 51. HATPIN. SEE PAGE 22

s, p, 3 d s, join p of centre r, 3 d s, p, 4 d s,—ch 3 d s, 7 p 3 d s bet, 3 d s. Continue around r, joining the circles together by two rings. Make 12 circles.

2d row—Clover leaves (c l), r, 4 d s, 7 p 2 d s bet, long p, 7 p 2 d s bet, 4 d s, centre r, 4 d s, 5 p 2 d s bet, join circle as shown in Fig. 50, 5 p 2 d s bet, 4 d s, repeat first r of c l. Ch 2 d s, 18 p 2 d s bet, 2 d s. R, 6 d s, join long p in c l, 7 p 2 d s bet,—last a long p—6 d s. Continue around.

3d row—R, 11 p 2 d s bet. Make 2 r, close. Join each pair of r to the one before, and to the last row as in Fig. 50.

4th row—4 r 9 d s p, 9 d s, close. Ch 8 p 2 d s bet; join last row and figures together as in the illustration.

Figure 51. Cover for Hatpin. — Use No. 10 crochet cotton, with continuous thread. Tie a knot

in threads. Ch sets of 5-5 sts making ch long enough for centre of cover, and sew the coil together on the wrong side. Finish the edge with little daisies of rings not joined, 9 long p, 1 d s between. Leave a short thread between rings. Sew to the coil by first and last p of each r and the thread between the rings. Cut a round piece of linen large enough to slip over a flat hatpin the size of the solid part of the tatting. Sew linen to edge of solid part of tatting, slip it over head of pin and draw up. Secure neatly. This hatpin cover and buckle to match, see Fig. 55, make novel ornaments for lingerie hats.

Figure 52. Border for Handkerchief.—Use No. 100 crochet cotton.

1st row—R 8 d s, p, 8 d s, ch 7, p, 3 d s between (bet), r 8 d s, join p in first r, 8 d s, r 8 d s p, 8 d s. Repeat rs and chs until corner is reached, when there is but one r, and the chs next to it join by 1st p.

2d row—Repeat the first row, joining as in the cut. At the corner make an extra ch and r, joining 3 r to the single r of the first row. When finished, add 2 r separately, beginning at the joining in the centre, joining by a p to the 3 r on each side.

3d row—Ch 7 p, 3 d s bet, join centre

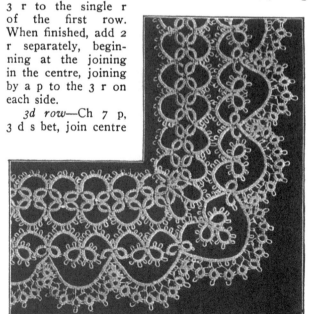

FIG. 52. HANDKERCHIEF CORNER. SEE PAGE 22

p to centre p of last ch; r 7 p, 3 d s bet; repeat r close to first r joining by last and first ps; ch 7 p, 3 d s bet, r 8 d s, join 5th p in previous r; 6 d s, small p, 2 d s; r 2 d s, join last r, 6 d s, p, 8 d s. At the corner make 3 r, 7 p, 3 d s bet, join the side rs together by the first p, and to centre r by second p.

4th row — Join thread between small rings of 3d row, ch 12 p, 3 d s between, join between next small rings. At corner, ch 16 p, 3 d s bet.

5th row — On each ch work 9 r, 3 p, 3 d s bet; on corner ch work 11 r, 3 p, 3 d s bet.

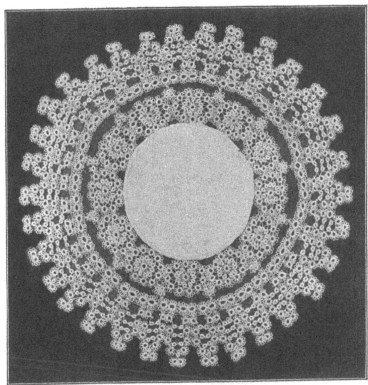

FIG. 53. DOILY. SEE PAGE 23

Figure 53. Doily.—*1st row*—12 circles; centre r, 1 d s, 11 p 2 d s between (bet), 1 d s. Double row small and larger rs; r 6 d s, join centre r, 6 d s, leave short thread, r 4 d s, 7 p 2 d s bet, 4 d s. Join circles by 2 r. Between circles add clover leaves (c l) of 3 d s, 5 p 2 d s bet, 3 d s. *2d row*—R 2 d s, 11 p 2 d s bet, 2 d s. Make two, and close, join pairs together and to the clover leaves, as in Fig. 53. *3d row* — With shuttle only; r, 4 d s, 7 p 2 d s bet, 4 d s, join 2d row, leave very short thread, make small r 6 d s, p, 6 d s. Make four large and three small rings; leave longer thread and make opposite large r; alternate as before, joining small rs to the 3 first made, and last large r to last row, close. Join figures by 3 large r. Add c l of 2 large r and 1 small r, the latter joining between outer large rs.

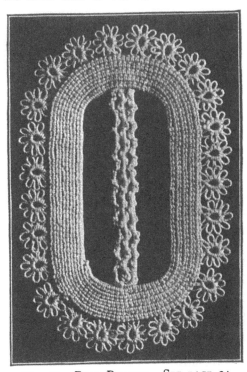

FIG. 54. BONBON BASKET
SEE PAGE 23

Figure 54. Bonbon Basket. — Made with crochet cotton No. 5. BOTTOM. — R 4 p s 2 d s between (bet),

make 4 r joined together by 1st and 4th p, and join last to first. Carry thread to 2d p of a r; r 3 p 3 d s bet, join next p of a centre r, leave a short thread, make another r joined to 3d p of last; continue until there is a circle of 12 r, joined together and to centre r. *Last row* — Repeat rs, making 19 or 20, and joining last row so that it will lie flat. SIDES. — R 3 p 3 d s bet; ch 3 p 3 d s bet; repeat r, join 2d p to 2d p of last r, and both, to base of a r of last row. Continue this row around, joining pairs of rs together, and to the next r but one of the last row. *2d row*—R 3 p 4 d s bet; ch 4 d s, join 1st p of ch of last row, 3 d s, join 2d p, 3 d s, join 3d p, 4 d s; repeat r, joining 2d p to 2d p of last r; continue around. Finish the top of basket with chs, 5 d s, p, 5 d s, join ps of last row; and shorter one, 5 d s, joining between two pairs of rs. Continue with the handle, r 5 d s, p, 5 d s; ch 6 d s, p, 6 d s; repeat r, join p of last r, make 6 pairs of rs and chs, join the other side of basket, then make chs only,

FIG. 55. BELT BUCKLE. SEE PAGE 24

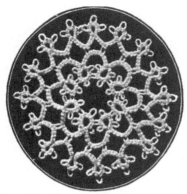

FIG. 56. CORNER MOTIF OF OCTAGON
INSERTION. SEE FIG. 58

joining between the pairs of rs across
the handle. To stiffen, see directions
for Fig. 41.

Figure 55. Belt Buckle. — Cut
from cardboard a buckle the size and
shape desired and wind it with smooth-
edge baby ribbon; wire the cardboard
if you want it very stiff. Make long
ch of No. 10 crochet cotton and sew
it on the buckle. To cover the centre
of buckle make sets of 5-5 sts, draw
the shuttle thread tight, and sew them
on. For the edge of the buckle, ring
9 p, 1 d s between, unjoined. Sew on
by first and last ps of rings and the
thread between rings.

Figure 58. Tea Cloth. (See details, Figs. 56, 57, 59, 60, 61, 62, 63, 64.)
—This elaborate tea-cloth is composed
of over 30 designs, and over 460 separate parts. Many of the beautiful
motifs can be adapted to a variety of
articles, as doilies, yokes, collars, ves-
tees, jabots, and many other uses.
Use spool cotton No. 30 or crochet
cotton No. 50.

FIG. 58. TEA CLOTH SEE
PAGE 24

FIG. 57. MOTIF FOR TRIANGLE NO. 1 IN
BORDER. SEE FIG. 58

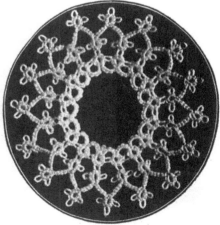

FIG. 59. MOTIF FOR TRIANGLE No. 2, IN BORDER.
SEE FIG. 58

CENTRE CIRCLE.—Make 16 r of 3 p
2 d s between (bet), joined together
at 1st p; and 16 ch of 4 d s. SECOND
CIRCLE.—Make 8 circles of 12 r, 3 p
2 d s bet, and 12 ch of 4 d s. Join
rings together, circles together by 2 p,
and circles to rs of centre circle, by
2 r of each circle. THIRD CIRCLE.—
Repeat 2d circle with 16 r, and join
the second circle by 2 r.

FOURTH CIRCLE. Fig. 60.—Make a
circle like the last, of 16 rs and chs,
then a double row, r, 3 p 2 d's bet,
joined by 2d p to a r of the circle;
ch, 5 d s, r, 3 p 2 d s bet. The
rs are not joined, but the motif is
joined by 2 r on each side to 2
motifs of the last circle.

HALF CIRCLE JOINING MOTIFS OF
FOURTH CIRCLE.—R, 3 p 3 d s bet;
join by mid-p to the motif, r next
the one joined to third circle on right
side; repeat chs and rs thrice, joining
in all 4 r of the motif. Add to the
last r a half circle of 11 rs and chs,
rs 3 p 2 d s bet, chs 4 d s; join last
r to 4th r of next motif, ch 4 d s,
r, join next r, repeat twice, close.

OBLONG MOTIFS OUTSIDE OF THE
FOURTH CIRCLE.—Two double rows of
14 r each. Rs 3 p 2 d s bet, joined,
chs 8 d s, p, 8 d s. Join 2 rows

SEE DETAILS FIGS. 56, 57, 59,
60, 61, 62, 63, 64

FIG. 60. FOURTH CIRCLE IN CENTRE.
SEE FIG. 58

FIG. 61. MOTIF CENTRE OF TRIANGLE NO. 2 IN
BORDER. SEE FIG. 58

together while working 2d row, and at end add 3 r.
Join as worked, 2 upper r of motif, skipping 1 r
of this motif between; and join 2 r of the half
circle at the end of this motif. A small clover leaf
(c l) fills the space at each side of the round
motif, between the oblong motif and the half
circle.

FIRST ROW OF QUADRANGLE.—5 rows of 5 circles
each. Make circles of 12 r, 1 d s, 3 p 2 d s bet,
1 d s; chs 2 d s. Join rs together, and circles together
by 2 p, and to the oblong motif by 2 p, skipping
one p between the circles.

2d row—R 2 d s, 3 ps 2 d s bet, 2 d s. Ch
3 d s.

3d row—R, 3 d s, 3 ps 2 d s bet, 3 d s; ch
3 d s.

4th row—4 d s, 3 p 3 d s bet, 4 d s, ch 4 d s.

5th row—4 d s, 3 p 4 d s bet, 4 d s; ch 4 d s.
Each row joined, by two r of each circle, to all
adjoining circles.

INSERTION OVER THE QUADRANGLE.—The narrow

bit over three circles. Of 19 rs and 18 chs. Rs
3 p 2 d s bet, joined together at 1st p; chs 4 d s.
Join outside circles by 1 r, the 3 inner circles by
2 r.

FIRST MOTIF OF PANEL BETWEEN QUADRANGLES.
—8 r, alternately 2 d s, p, 6 d s, p, 6 d s, p, 2 d s,
and 2 d s, p, 4 d s, p, 4 d s, p, 2 d s; join together
and at the close.

Second Motif.—4 c l, with chs between of 6 d s.
First r 6 d s, p, 4 d s, p, 2 d s; centre r 2 d s,
join 1st r, 6 d s, p, 6 d s, p, 2 d s; third r like
first, join centre r; join leaves by mid-ps.

Third Motif—As the last, except chs 8 d s, and
leaves increased 4 d s.

Fourth Motif—R, 15 p 1 d s bet, close. Double
row—Inner rs, 15, of 3 p 2 d s bet, joined to the
r, and together; outer rs, 15, of 3 p 4 d s bet.

INSERTION AROUND PANEL.—R, 3 p 4 d s bet;
ch 4 d s, p, 4 d s. At inner end two small c l are
added, and another one between those the first
motif. At the outer end, add 6 clover leaves around
the largest motif. Join motifs and insertion as made,
and insertion to the quadrangles.

INSERTION DEFINING THE OCTAGON.—See Fig. 62,
in which two outer rows are omitted. Of 7 rows.

1st row—R, 3 p 3 d s bet; ch 3 d s, p, 3 d s.

2d row—R 5 p 2 d s bet; ch 5 p 2 d s bet.

FIG. 63. MEDALLION ON EDGE. SEE FIG. 58

3d row—R 5
p 2 d s bet;
ch 2 p 2 d s
bet; r 5 p 2
d s bet.

4th row —
Repeat 3d row.

5th row —
Repeat 2d row.

*6th and 7th
rows* — Repeat
1st row.

INSERTION
CORNER MOTIF.

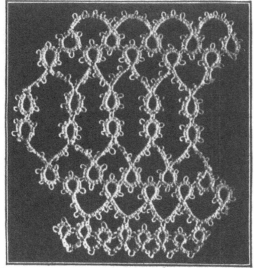

FIG. 62. INSERTION DEFINING THE OCTAGON.
SEE FIG. 58

FIG. 64. EDGING OF LINEN INSETS.
SEE FIG. 58

(See Fig. 56.) *1st row*—8 rs and chs, rs joined together. R 5 p 2 d s bet; ch 2 p 4 d s bet. *2d row*—R 3 p 2 d s bet, unjoined; ch 4 d s, join, 4 d s. Join two ch to each ch of the row before. Make the 8 motifs first, and in making the insertion join the motifs to it as shown in the complete pattern.

ROUND MOTIF FOR TRIANGLE 1. (See Fig. 57.)—Centre r, 12 p 1 d s bet. A double row of small and larger r, 12 each. Small, 4 d s join p of r 4 d s; larger 3 ps 4 d s bet, join together.

3d row—R 5 p 2 d s bet, ch 5 d s, join r of last row, 5 d s.

4th row—R 2 d s, p, 2 d s, join 4th p of r in last row, 2 d s, p, 2 d s, join 2d p of next r; 2 d s, p, 2 d s, ch 3 d s, 5 p 2 d s bet, 3 d s. Make 10 motifs joined together as shown in Fig. 58.

OVAL MOTIF FOR TRIANGLE 2. (Fig. 59.) *Centre*—10 rs and chs. R 3 p 2 d s bet, join together; ch 4 d s. *Outer row*—R 5 d s, 2 d s bet; ch, 5 p 2 d s bet. Join rs in groups of 3, and to the centre circle as shown in the cut. Ch 8 d s, p, 4 d s; c l, 1st r, 4 d s, join ch, 2 p 4 d s bet; centre r, 4 d s join 1st r, 5 d s, p, 5 d s, p, 4 d s; 3d r as the 1st; ch 4 d s, join c l, 8 d s.

TRIANGULAR MOTIF.—Centre of triangle 2. (Fig. 61.) *Centre Circle* of 5 rs and chs. R, 5 p 2 d s bet; ch 3 p 4 d s bet.

2d row—R 3 p 2 d s bet; ch 5 p 2 d s bet. Join three r, each to a p of 1 ch of last row, continue around.

3d row—There are c l at the three points; and 6 groups of 3 joined rs; each group joined to 2 ch at points of the last row, the centre r unjoined; and a ch between each pair of groups. Rs 5 p 2 d s bet; chs the same, except the longer joining chs of 7 p; chs to c l 9 d s; c l 3 p 4 d s bet, join rs together.

MEDALLION ON EDGE. (Fig. 63.)—Centre, a square of four c l and chs. C l rs joined, leaves joined together. Rs 3 p 4 d s bet, centre r, 5 d s bet on top; chs 7 d s.

2d row—R 5 p 1 d s bet; ch 3 d s, p, 3 d s. Join rs together. Join each 7th ch to the centre p of a c l of 1st row.

3d row—R 3 p 2 d s bet; ch 5 d s, p, 5 d s. Join each r to a r of 2d row.

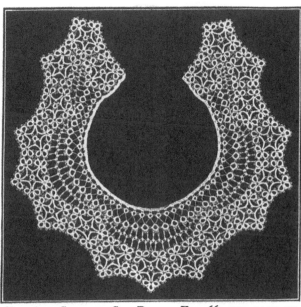

FIG. 65. COLLAR. SEE DETAIL FIG. 66, AND PAGE 27

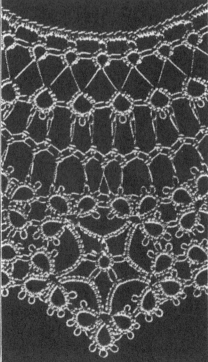

FIG. 66. DETAIL OF COLLAR FIG. 65

4th row—Ch 6 d s, p, 6 d s; join each ch to a ch of the row before.

CENTRE MEDALLION ON EDGE.—Repeat the last medallion, but in the last row add rs of 3 p 3 d s bet. Join the 3 motifs together by 3 chs.

The linen insets may all be made first, with a very narrow hem, edged on three sides with the first row of the edging, then sewed to the octagon. The second row of the edging joins to the insets, the triangles between, and the large motifs on the edge.

EDGING ON LINEN INSETS. (Fig. 64.) *1st row*—R 3 p 2 d s bet; ch 4 d s, p, 4 d s, join the rings together. The 2d row should not be added until all is ready to be joined together.

2d row—C l, r 5 p 3 d s bet; ch the same, single r the same. Join c ls by second ps to the single r between, and the chs together by the first ps. Join to the first row by 2 p over single r, the next p but one, and the first on next ch, and repeat. At the point between the linen insets, reverse a c l and join to the 1st row, and join 2 opposite single r, together. Join the motifs together as shown in the completed work Fig. 58.

Figure 65. Collar. (See detail, Fig 66.)—Use crochet cotton No. 15.

MEDALLIONS.—Centre r, 5 p 2 d s between (bet). Clover leaf (c l); r 4 d s, 5 p 2 d s bet, 4 d s; join r together. Ch 7 d s, join p of centre r, 7 d s. Make 5 each, c ls and chs; join c ls together by 2d ps. Join medallions together as shown in Fig. 66.

Upper row—Alternate small and larger rs, leaving about ¼-inch of thread between. Small r, 3 d s, 3 p 2 d s bet, 3 d s. Larger r, 4 d s, 5 p 2 d s bet, 4 d s. Crochet a ch for the neck with 3 ch between ps; cover the ch with double crochet. Baste the collar on stiff paper, and fill the spaces as shown in Fig. 66. Go over these with plain fagoting, turn and work back, two buttonhole sts on each st of fagoting, alternating on sides of centre. In the small spaces of the fronts use only one buttonhole-st.

Figure 67. Tatted Cords.—The upper cord is made of 6 single sts like the first half of

27

a d s, then 6 like the last half of a d s. This is one set of sts, the term is one set of 6-6 sts. Repeat to required length. *The middle cord is made in the same way with a p after each set. The lower cord with a p at centre and end of each set.*

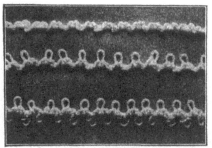

FIG. 67. TATTED CORDS. SEE PAGE 27

crochet cotton on the shuttle, and two balls of No. 50 crochet cotton. With the heavy thread between the two others, tie them and hold the knot between the left thumb and finger. Wind the two ball threads as usual around the left fingers a little apart. Ch 1 d s with the upper thread; turn the work half way around *toward* you, ch 1 d s with the lower thread; turn the work back *from* you, and repeat. Be careful to turn the work always the same way, and only half way around, and there will be no tangling. Keep a firm tension on the threads. Picots may be added as in the next cord.

THE THIRD CORD.—Has ps and padded rings. A second shuttle is used, with padding cord for the rings; let this cord lie along the under side of the work; make rings over it, of 10 d s, draw closely. Carry the padding to the next r. When finished it may be sewed under the cord, or cut close to the rs.

Figure 70. Padded Cords.—Wind four strands of No. 5 crochet cotton on the shuttle, and use two balls of crochet cotton No. 30, the thread wound on left fingers a little way apart to keep from tangling. Join the 3 threads and hold knot between left thumb and finger. Ch 3 d s, p, 1 d s with the upper thread on the left hand; turn the work half way around *toward* you, ch 3 d s, p, 1 d s with the lower thread; turn the work back *from* you. Turn the same way always, and only half way around. Repeat to the

Figure 68. Padded Tatting Cords.—These are made by using a heavy thread on the shuttle, a lighter one on the ball.

THE UPPER CORD.— There are 4 strands of No. 5

length desired.

The lower cord is made with two shuttles and a ball. Begin as the upper cord, omitting the ps. After 4 d s with the first shuttle, leave a short thread, with the thread shuttle make a r of 4 d s, p, 4 d s; leave short thread, turn, ch 4 d s; turn, ch 4 d s; r 4 d s, p, 4 d s. Repeat. Four strands of No. 5 crochet cotton were used for padding.

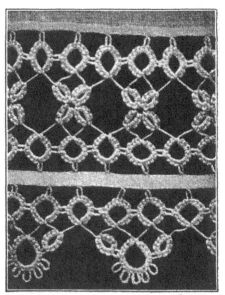

FIG. 69. DETAIL OF APRON FIG. 71

Figure 71. Apron with Tatting. (See detail, Fig. 69.) — Use crochet cotton No. 30.

EDGING. — Fig. 69 is made with the shuttle only. A double row; r 5 d s, p, 5 d s; leave a short thread; r 3 p 4 d s between (bet), leave thread; large r, 5 d s, join small r, 6 p 2 d s bet, 5 d s; r 4 d s, join, 2 p 4 d s bet. Repeat. INSERTION.—Also with but one thread. R 4 d s, p, 4 d s, leave short thread; r 3 p 4 d s bet; r 4 d s, join first r, 4 d s, leave short thread; r 3 p 4 d s bet. Repeat. Make another double row, join to this by ps of the two small r, the four r all join the p of the first r. Join edging and insertion by a narrow braid, sewed on.

Figure 72. Scarf.—The length of the scarf is the width of the net, 2 yards. Get ¾ of a yard if a hem is desired, or finish with tatted edge. Even off the edges to leave 24 inches. Put 1-inch hem on the ends. Wind shuttle with No. 30 crochet cotton. Without cutting from ball, knot (k) thread into net at the hem. Ch 7 d s, join into edge of scarf, a little more than ¼ inch from first k. Continue along the edge, fastening at regular intervals of ¼ inch. Take in a little less than ¼ inch of the net, or two of the meshes, to make a firm edge in place of a hem. Make 10 small medallions joined together by the small picots and 5 larger. Unwind ½ yard of thread from shuttle. R 4 d s, 1 small p, 3 d s, 5

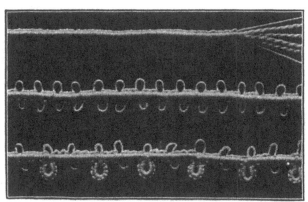

FIG. 68. PADDED CORDS. SEE PAGE 28

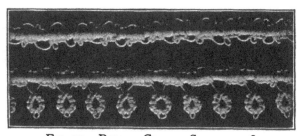

FIG. 70. PADDED CORDS. SEE PAGE 28

longer p, 3 d s, 1 small p, 4 d s, close. Ch 2 d s, make 6 r and 6 ch, join rings, tie. This completes the small medallion.

For the large medallions, unwind 3 yards of the thread from shuttle. Make small medallion as before. K thread between 1st and 6th rings. Ch 4 d s, 9 p, 2 d s between (bet) 4 d s, k between next 2 r. Repeat over each r. Now lay the net over the outline of design traced on stiff paper, and pin firmly in place. Pin the medallions in the positions marked for them. Take the net from the pattern and sew each medallion to the net, in the centre, leaving the upper part of rings free to slip ends of chs under, that form vines and tendrils. Pin the net over the tracing again with the medallions in the proper position. Tie k in thread. Make ch about 10 inches long, pin it on one of the vines to exactly the right length, tie and cut threads about ½ inch from k. Baste ch, carefully following the tracing. Sew over and under the chain, not through it, so as not to pull it out of place. Make all the vines required, measuring and basting each one made. When all are on one end of scarf loosen from pattern and sew to the net, catching the under side of the chs, with no stitches on the upper side of chs. Be careful neither to stretch nor pucker the net. When vines are sewed on, pin work on the pattern, k the thread; unwind about 1 yard from the shuttle, for tendrils; make ch about 3 inches long. Measure, tie and cut, leaving about ½ inch of thread. Fasten ends of ch next to the medallions, under the rings left loose, drawing the ends of thread through to the wrong side. Pin and baste all tendrils in place, curling the chs to fit

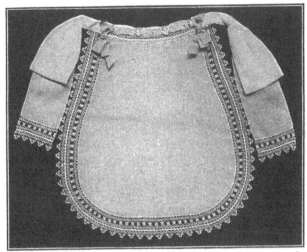

FIG. 71. APRON. SEE DETAIL FIG. 69, AND PAGE 28

each tracing. Remove from pattern and sew on all the medallions (wrong side), around the rs and outside chains. You now have a very handsome scarf, but if a more elaborate one is desired, add rings of three sizes, the largest at lower corners: r 3 p 6 d s bet; second, 3 p 5 d s bet; smallest, 3 p 4 d s bet. For centre vines use rings of 3 p 4 d s between. Leave an inch or more of the thread on each ring. Place rings on the vine, draw the threads through the net, tie, and sew through the knot and carefully fasten the threads to the vine on the wrong side; cut ends close and sew on the ring. Press over a damp cloth, with a cloth over it, when scarf is finished. Place rings as suggested by the illustration.

Figure 73. Jabot. (See Fig. 74.)—Made with No. 12 spool cotton, or crochet cotton No. 50 or 60. *First rosette*—Wind 5 yds thread on the shuttle; use continuous thread. R 7 d s, p, 7 d s; ch 3 d s, 5 p 2 d s between, 3 d s; r 7 d s, join p of 1st r, 7 d s. Make five r and four ch, join all r to p of first r. Ch connecting stars, 5 d s, 7 p 2 d s

FIG. 72. SCARF IN TATTED APPLIQUÉ ON NET. SEE PAGE 28

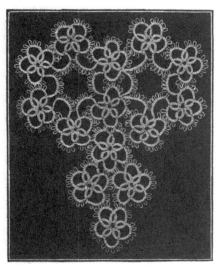

FIG. 73. JABOT. SEE FIG. 74, AND PAGE 29

four stars. Join mid-p of the fourth ch of the fourth star to mid-p of 3d ch of a star, and the connecting ch, between 3d and 4th ch of same star. Join another connecting ch, between first two ch of next star, and a third ch to the beginning of second rosette.

CENTRE CROSSPIECE. (See Fig. 74.) — Make one of the rosette stars, complete with 5 chs; ch, 9 d s, 5 p 2 d s between (bet), 9 d s; join between the next 2 ch; ch 15 d s, 5 p 2 d s bet, 15 d s, join where last ch begins, close. This forms the upper end. At the lower end, join the mid-p of a lower ch; ch 4 d s, 5 p 2 d s bet, 4 d s; join mid-p of the other lower ch; ch 9 d s, 5 p 2 d s bet, 9 d s; join at beginning of the last ch, close. Sew with fine thread, and a few buttonhole sts, to the upper and lower ps of the two centre stars.

PENDANT.— Make four complete stars separately, one-yard of shuttle thread for each. *Upper star* —Join second ch to the star at the left, and the centre star of the jabot; see cut. Join third ch to correspond. In the fifth ch make but 4 p. *2d star*— To the right; join fourth ch, last two p, to two ps of lower ch, first star; join fifth ch, first

between, 5 d s. Repeat five times joining the first ch of each star to last ch of the one before by mid-ps; a n d connecting chains, by 1st p to last p of the ch before, and the last ch, also by the last p to the 1st p of the first ch. *Second rosette* — F o u r yards of shuttle thread. Make only four stars.

2 p, to next ps of first star. *3d star*—At left side; join 4th ch, last 2 p, to 2 p of left ch, first star; join 5th ch, first 2 p to ps on lower ch of first star, next 2 p to next ps on second star. *4th star*—Lowest; join 4th ch, 3d and 4th ps to 2d and 3d ps of ch of 3d star; 5th ch 2d and 3d ps to 2d and 3d ps on ch of 2d star. A small rose of Irish crochet on the crosspiece centre adds a dainty finish; and colored ribbons, or black velvet, or colored velvet, through the openings completes it.

FIG. 74. CROSS-PIECE OF JABOT FIG. 73

Figure 75. Alphabet.

A — Begin at the top, continue down inner right side. R 5 p 2 d s between (bet); ch 16 d s, p, 20 d s, small p; r 3 d s, p, 3 d s, join small p, repeat r, join same p, forming the base of the stem at the right. Ch, 2 p 4 d s bet, join 11th d s of the 20 d s ch; repeat ch, join p; ch 4 d s, p, 4 d s, join 9th d s of 16 ch; repeat ch, join r. Ch 16 d s, p, form bar across to stem by 8 d s, join p on opposite side, 8 d s, join p on left stem. Ch 20 d s, p, 6 p 4 d s bet, 2 d s, join 2 d s before the 3d p back; ch 2 p, 4 d s bet; join at 1st p; repeat ch, join half way to bar; repeat ch, join bar; ch 4 d s, p, 4 d s, join midway to r, repeat ch, join r, close.

B — Make a stem like the right one of "A" reversed, and at base but one r of 5 p 3 d s bet. Returning to top r, ch 28 d s, p, 8 d s, join mid-p on stem, 8 d s, join last p, forming the bar. Ch 35 d s, join base of stem; turn, ch 2 p 4 d s bet, join 10th d s of long ch; ch p, 4 d s, 2 p 4 d s bet; join 22d d s; repeat ch 3 times without the p at beginning — the last time with but 2 d s at last — joining at mid-p, 10th d s and 18th d s; ch 2 d s, 2 p 4 d s bet, join 1st r and close.

C — Make the top r 5 p 2 d s bet; ch 35 d s, p, 40 d s, small p, 2 d s, p, 2 d s, join small p, making r at lower end. Ch 2 d s, p, 4 d s, p, 4 d s, join 9th d s of 40 ch; ch p, 4 d s p, 4 d s, join 17th d s; ch p, 2 p, 4 d s bet, join 27th d s; ch p, 3 p, 4 d s bet,

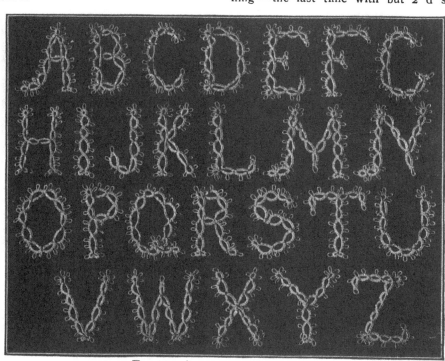

FIG. 75. ALPHABET. SEE PAGE 30

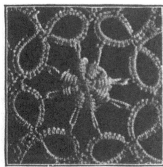

FIG. 76. DETAIL OF FIGS. 78 AND 79

join p; ch 2 p 4 d s, join 13th d s; ch p, 4 d s, p, 4 d s, p, 2 d s, join 21st d s; ch 2 d s, p, 4 d s, p, 4 d s, join 29th d s; ch p, 3 d s, p, 3 d s, join the 1st r, close.

D —Stem as that of "B." Ch 28 d s, p, 35 d s, join base of stem. Ch 2 p 4 d s bet, join 10th d s; repeat ch 4 times, joining 22d, mid-p, 9th and 18th d s, the last with but 2 d s after last p; ch 2 d s, p, 4 d s, p, 4 d s, close.

E — Make upper r; continue to the right; ch 16 d s, p, 7 d s, small p, 2 d s, p 2 d s, join small p, forming small r at end of the top. Ch 4 d s, p, 4 d s, join p; ch p, 4 d s, p, 4 d s, join 9th d s; ch 4 d s, p, 4 d s, join r. Make stem as in "B," but between the chs of 16 and 20 d s, add p, 5 d s, p, 3 d s, p, 3 d s; join p before the last; 3 d s, p, 3 d s, join same p, 5 d s, join 1st p. Continue down the stem, then repeat the upper bar reversed.

F.—Make like "E," but omit the lower bar, and for the r at base of stem, two small r of 3 d s, p, 3 d s.

G — Like "C," add at lower end two instead of one small r of 3 d s, p, 3 d s.

H — Make two stems as in "F," joined in the centre by a ch of 16 d s, join, 8 d s, join 9th d s, 8 d s, join beginning of the ch.

I — A single stem as that of "F."

J — Ring and 4 links as in "I," add 2 links and a tiny r as at the end of "C."

K—Stem as in "F," close. R and 2 links joined at mid-p of stem, 2 links and a r joined at mid-p of stem, close.

L — As the stem and lower part of "E."

M—The left stem as that of "A." After joining r at the top, ch 16 d s. p, 10 d s, p, 10 d s, p, 16 d s; repeat r and make stem like the right stem of "A." After joining r, make 2 ch of 8 d s, joining middle and end of 16 ch; one of 10 d s, join p between chs of 10 d s. Make a loop of 6 d s, small p, 2 d s, p, 2 d s, join small p, 6 d s, join beginning of loop. Continue chs to the first r, close.

N — As "M," omitting the right stem.

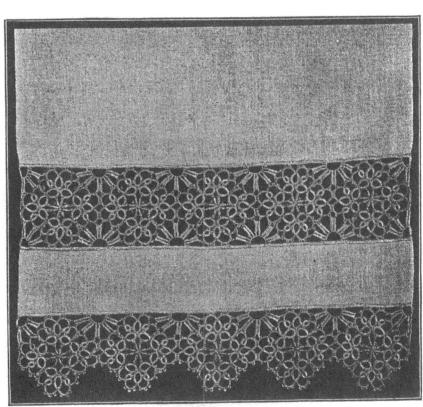

FIG. 77. DETAIL OF FIGS. 78 AND 79

O — Ch 50 d s, small p, 50 d s, join in a r and make chs, joining as in others.

P — A stem like "A," but with ps on both sides of the 2 lower links. The circle as the upper part of "B," but 2 upper links larger.

Q — Like "O"; add a r, 2 links, and a r.

R — As "P," with 2 links and a r added.

S — A ring, small link, 2 a little larger, and 6 larger links, repeat r at the end.

T—As "F" in the stem and right bar; omit the top r, add the left bar, and pull into shape.

U — Make a r, down the inner left side ch 90 d s, repeat r, make 9 links of 2 p 4 d s between, joining at 10th d s, join r, close.

V — Like the right stem of "A," with a left one continued from the 2 little r at the base.

W—As "V" in the stems, "M" in the centre.

X—A stem like that of "B," but with 5 links. R, and ch of 5 links with a r at the other end. Repeat r, make 2 links, join the stem after the first 2 links, make 3 links and r.

Y—As the rings and centre of "M," continued from the joining as the left stem of "A."

Z—Begin at the upper right corner, make r, then top of the letter as in "F," with one more link, join r; ch 40 d s, repeat r; repeat the upper part reversed, join r; ch 8 d s, join 8th d s of 40 ch. Make 5 links in all, joining 8th d s; join r, close.

As tatting will vary, judgment must be used in number and length of

FIG. 78. LIBRARY SCARF. SEE DETAILS FIGS. 76 AND 77, AND PAGE 32

links to make the letters even. Pull them into shape while making, and press carefully afterwards. These letters are very effective on table pieces and towels.

Figure 78. Library Scarf. (See details, Figs. 76, 77.)—Use No. 3 crochet cotton. The model scarf was in écru. The tatted medallions are joined together by weaving, see Figs. 76 and 77.

MEDALLION.—* R 7 d s, 3 p 5 d s between (bet), 7 d s; ch, 4 d s, 3 p 3 d s bet, 4 d s; r 5 d s, join last p of r, 2 d s, p, 5 d s; repeat ch; r 7 d s, join last p of small r, 5 d s, join mid-p in first r, 5 d s, p, 7 d s. Repeat ch and small r; repeat ch and large r, joining by mid-ps to the two other large r *. Before repeating the ch make another large r. Repeat between stars thrice, and join the first r.

CENTRE OF MEDALLION. (See Fig. 76.)—With a large needle and 1¼ yards of thread, using the 8 centre ps for foundation, weave 6 times around, close to the centre, putting the needle under 2 strands at a time, and going over again the last strand, forming a heavy r on the upper side. Finish with a French knot in centre of the right side, and catch the threads down close on the wrong side. Join medallions by 2 p each, of 2 pairs of chs adjoining. Join to the linen by two chs and weaving between.

FOR THE WEAVING. (See Fig. 77.)—After sewing the medallions to the linen, make a 1-inch loop with the thread on the linen between them. Carry thread through the 1st p and back to the loop, join; repeat to next p, back and join; repeat around, forming ten strands, and weave over each pair back and forth, loosely but evenly.

Figure 79. Pillow with Weaving.—The materials for this pillow are the same as those used for the scarf, Fig. 78, page 31. Make the bands of insertion according to directions for the library scarf, Fig. 78, with directions on page 32. THE EDGING, Fig. 80, is made as one-fourth of a medallion, adding a joining ch of 1 d s, 3 p 2 d s between, 1 d s; and joining the scallops by 2 p of adjoining chains.

Figure 81. Edging.—R, 9 d s, p, 1 d s, p, 9 d s. Opposite r, 5 d s, p, 3 d s, p, 7 d s; ch 8 d s, p, 8

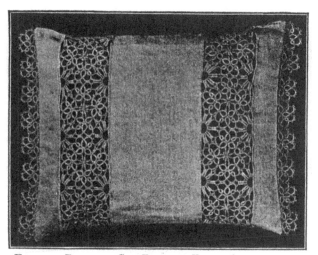

FIG. 79. PILLOW. SEE DETAILS FIGS. 76. 77, AND 80, AND PAGE 32

FIG. 81. EDGING. SEE PAGE 32

d s; r 10 d s, join 1st r, 1 d s, p, 8 d s, p, 2 d s. Draw up very close to r and make r of 2 d s, join last r, 9 d s, p, 4 d s, p, 5 d s, p, 7 d s; ch 7 d s; r 3 d s, join last r, 7 d s, 3 p 3 d s between, 7 d s, p, 3 d s; ch 7 d s; r 7 d s, join last r, 5 d s, p, 4 d s, p, 9 d s, p, 2 d s; r 2 d s, join last r, 8 d s, p, 1 d s, 10 d s; ch 8 d s, join opposite ch, 8 d s. Repeat the first pair of r. joining the first to mid-p of last r, and the second to mid-p of the small upper r; ch 7 d s, p, 3 d s, p, 7 d s. Repeat from the beginning.

Figure 82. Collar. (See details, Figs. 83, 84, 85, 86.)—Baste the lace net smoothly on the pattern and leave while making.

To make edge, use No. 40 crochet cotton on shuttle and No. 60 for second thread. Join threads, chain 4 d s, 9 p separated by 2 d s, 3 d s, form loop by crossing ch of stitches, 1 d s from beginning, shuttle thread over, ball thread under ch. Draw shuttle thread close, continue with 2 d s, 7 p separated by 2 d s, 5 d s, 9 p separated by 2 d s, form another loop. Repeat, making length to reach

FIG. 80. EDGING FOR PILLOW FIG. 79

around collar, neck included. Press this edge flat with warm iron; baste on edge of collar, placing it with outer edge of scallops even with edge of net. Sew to net all around collar with fine thread.

The next row is joined to 2 ps between scallops of last row, being careful to take in edge of net. Work five sets of 5-5 stitches to each scallop, after joining leave a p when beginning next scallop. Omit around the neck.

Last row—Join to ps between scallops of row just made. Work 7 p 2 d s between (bet), join to next p between scallops.

SOLID COILS. (See Fig. 85.)—Wind No. 40 cotton around shuttle a few times. Tie a single knot in thread, between shuttle and ball. Take knot between thumb and finger, shuttle thread towards you. Pass ball thread around hand as usual and, for convenience, while beginning work, pass shuttle thread around little finger and back between thumb and finger. Work 12 d s, leaving a short p between the knot and first st. Now drop thread from little finger and draw shuttle thread through sts to the knot at beginning of the coil. Continue d s, drawing shuttle thread tight so as to form the coil as worked. Hold closely, making the open space left in centre as small as possible. When two rows are worked, it will be easier if each row is sewed in place, as made. In last row of coil leave a p after each 3d d s.

Scrolls are begun in same manner as coils, but left open, with a p at each 5 d s, after the first 12 d s.

Clover leaves are made of the cross loops of more or less p in number in same manner as edge of collar.

ROSES. (See Fig. 86.) —Number 40 cotton, make a ring of 24 p separated by 1½ d s. Close, making a r as small as possible. Carry the thread to 1st p, join ball thread, work ch, 7 p 2 d s bet, join in same p. Carry the threads to 4 p from last joining, repeat ch, join as before. Continue around r, making six loops, which forms first row of petals. Carry the threads to p at left of first petal, work 3 d s, 11 p 2 d s bet,

of rose opposite first set; sew the 2d p in scroll to p between next two petals of rose. Make third set of scrolls, join the 2d p of scroll to the next space between petals of rose and join at 3d p to centre of next rose petal; ch 3 p, 6 d s, join mid-p of next upper rose petal; ch 3 p, join 5th p on first scroll; ch 3 p, join next 3d p of scroll; ch 3 p, 12 d s, join centre of rose as did the first scroll. Make other half of set in same manner.

With No. 60 ball thread and No. 40 shuttle thread work two rows scallops around whole motif, making scallops of 7 p 2 d s bet, and joining at convenient intervals to work already made, to keep shape of pattern. Join second row to p between scallops of first

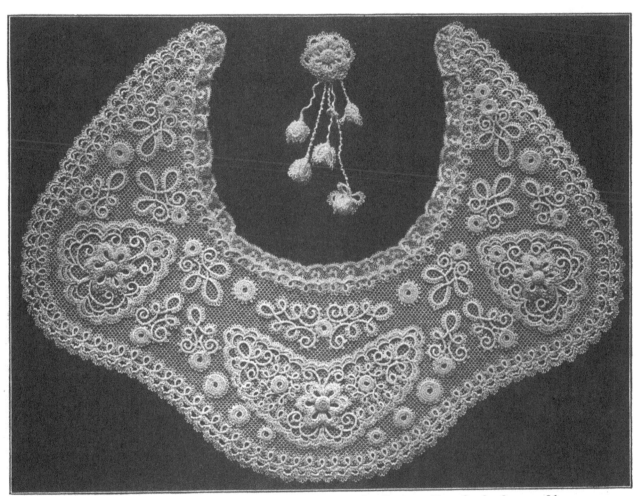

FIG. 82. COLLAR IN TATTING APPLIQUÉ ON NET, AND JABOT. SEE DETAILS FIGS. 83, 84, 85, AND 86, AND PAGE 32

3 d s, join to 1st p at right of first petal. Repeat all around for second row of petals. Carry the threads to remaining p between petals of second row, 3 d s, 17 p separated by 2 d s, 3 d s, join p between next two petals. Repeat all around, join last petal to same p as first petal, make four roses. Small flat crocheted balls are used for the centre of roses.

HEART-SHAPED MOTIF ON SHOULDER. — Cut paper pattern. Baste rose in centre. Make three sets of scrolls as before described, with 6 d s between p, 8 p in each scroll. Join one set of scrolls between petals of rose toward point of pattern. Make coil of three rows, join between the scrolls at point of pattern. Another set of scrolls of 9 p meeting between petals

row, changing the size of scallops to fit evenly.

CRESCENT-SHAPED MOTIF AT BACK. — Cut paper pattern of crescent 5 inches in length from point to point, and 2¼ inches deep in centre. Baste rose in centre of pattern. Make two coil wheels thus: A coil of three rows, last row having a p after each 4th d s, making 9 p around coil. After sewing rows in place, join threads to 1st p made; turn, work 7 d s close to joining, 7 p 2 d s bet, 3 d s, form loop by crossing ch at 3 d s from 1st p; work 4 d s, join ball thread to next p on coil; continue around coil.

Baste these wheels on each side of rose. Sew two loops of wheel to two outside petals of rose. For clover-leaf (c l) scroll at each end, begin scroll as before, making a p after each 6 d s. At 4th p join third loop on crescent wheel from loop joined to the rose. At next p of scroll join next loop on wheel 1 p from centre. Work 6 d s, p, 12 d s, 9 p 2 d s bet, 3 d s, form first leaf of clover by crossing ch at point 3 d s from 1st p. Work 12 d s, 17 p 2 d s bet, 3 d s, form second and third leaves like first. Make opposite scroll like first one, join opposite scroll, also at loop on other side of centre one, and also the next loop, as in first scroll. At top of rose work two scrolls, join at 2d p to outer petal of rose; join at 3d p to first loop in wheel from rose; 4 p 6 d s bet, bring end of scroll to rose between petals at top, the opposite one finishing at same point.

At bottom of rose make two more scrolls, each joining at second and third p of scroll to p

FIG. 84. ROSEBUD FOR JABOT. SEE FIG. 82, AND PAGE 34

at side of two petals of rose. After making four more p and 6 d s, with shuttle thread make tiny r, joining second p of scroll and petal of rose, ch 3 ps, 12 d s, bring ch to centre of petal at bottom as at top of rose and finish ends. Work all around motif a row of scallops and loops, join ps of work already made, making the loops larger or smaller as required. Work another row of scallops around outside of last row, joining between scallops of last row.

CLOVER-LEAF, COIL, AND SCROLL MOTIF. (See Figs. 82, 83.) —Make coil of three rows, making p at each 3d d s of last row of coils, scroll of 12 d s, 9 p, with 5 d s between, 7th p joined to a p on coil, 12 d s after last p. Leaf of 21 p, 2 d s between, followed by 12 d s. Middle leaf of 25 p, 12 d s, and third leaf like first. Nine d s joined to last p made in scroll, finish as on opposite side.

Six motifs are required of this size, also six more made in same manner, except that the two side leaves of the clover have 19 instead of 21 p. Sew a second smaller coil to two of the larger motifs for extreme ends of collar.

The motif above crescent at back has a coil, in centre of two sets of scrolls with which are made five-leaf clovers, first leaf having 15 p, second leaf 11 p, centre leaf 17 p.

FIG. 85. COILS FOR COLLAR FIG. 82

The six coils around bottom of crescent are graduated in size, having two, three, and four rows. The other four separate coils having 4 rows each, and all separate coils having 2 d s between ps instead of 3 like those attached to motifs.

Before sewing to net, place all work on flannel, right side down, cover with damp cloth, press with hot iron, then baste to position through both net and paper pattern; then with No. 100 thread sew around all edges to net, also through the centre of large motifs, fasten each centre end of coil and scroll through the small p at the beginning of each.

ROSEBUDS AND STEMS FOR JABOT. (See Fig. 84.) —Make chains of sets of stitches, drawing shuttle thread close enough to twist

FIG. 83. FULL-SIZE DETAIL OF THE CENTRE BACK OF COLLAR. SEE DETAILS FIGS. 85 AND 86

FIG. 86. FIRST ROW OF ROSE IN COLLAR FIG. 82. SEE FIG. 83

slightly, then at end of chains a cluster of four loops for petals with ps around edge, longer at centre of loops. Make small crocheted balls, fill with cotton, sew in centre of petal cluster, catch petals around the ball. A second cluster of petals may be made, having four loops, giving the effect of a bud opening. Sew stems to under side of rose to join ends of collar in front.

By sewing a row of narrow lace inside of tatted edge around neck, the collar will be protected and improved.

Figure 87. Change Purse.

Materials. — One ball of white crochet silk, a bunch of steel beads No. 9, and an ivory ring.

String four or five hundred beads on ball thread; this is as many as can be conveniently handled in working, more may be added. Fill shuttle from same ball, slipping the beads along as the shuttle is filled. Tie a single knot in silk, and make a p at the beginning. Full directions will be found on page 19, Fig. 44, and also for making sets of stitches.

TOP OF PURSE. — Work one set of 5-5 sts, p, 1 set with p at centre, to turn downward opposite the first p; draw shuttle thread tight; work 2 sets of 5-5 sts without a p; 2 sets with p at beginning and centre of each set, making 2 p on each side of cord. Work 2 sets without p, then 2 sets with p. Continue until there are 12 spaces between ps and 11 pairs of p on each side of the cord. Work 1 set with p at beginning and centre, join the p at beginning of the work. This is the twelfth pair of p, and completes the circle at the opening of the purse. Carry threads to 1st p at right of joining.

1st row — * Work 3 d s, p, 3 d s, a p of 3 beads;—slip the beads close to the last sts;— 3 d s, p, 3 d s; join 1st p on ch. Work 1 d s, p with one bead, 1 d s, join 2d p of same pair on ch *. Repeat between stars around, and first scallop.

2d row — Carry threads to p on side of

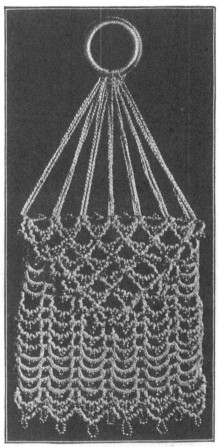

FIG. 87. CHANGE PURSE. SEE PAGE 35

first scallop; repeat the first row, but with 4 d s.

3d, 4th, and 5th rows—Like the second row.

The next four rows are alike; of 1 set 5-5 sts, p, 2 sets 4-4 sts, p of 3 beads, 2 sets 4-4 sts, p, 1 set 5-5 sts, join side p of scallop; bar of 1 d s, p of 1 bead, 1 d s; join side p of next scallop.

The next four rows are like the first, but with 5 d s between side ps and centre.

The next row closes the bottom of the purse. Hold the two sides together and join the ps of both at the same time, with sets of sts and bar as in four middle rows. Turn, and work back across the six scallops of the bottom, 5 sets of 4-4 sts and a p of 3 beads in the centre, to each scallop and a 3-beaded p between scallops.

Work the last row with 3 sets 4-4 sts, p of 12 beads, 3 sets 4-4 sts; join at beaded p between scallops, and leave there a p of 12 beads.

To FINISH THE TOP OF PURSE. —Join back, left side, 1st pair of p, upper side of cord. Work around the purse one row like the first row after the top circle. Work a second row across back of sets 4-4 sts. After the sixth scallop turn and work back, making 5 sets with a beaded p at centre; join between scallops of last row without the beaded connection. Carry threads to beaded p at top of last scallop made, work 2 sets 4-4 sts, p of 3 beads, 2 sets 4-4 sts, join beaded p of next scallop, work across, joining to the beaded p of each scallop, which diminishes the number of scallops by one. Next row back, work over each scallop and join between scallops. Carry thread to beaded p at top of scallop, work across, join beaded ps as before. Each row from left to right has one less scallop, but from right to left the number is the same as the row before. Continue until scallops are worked off to one. Tie and sew ends.

Beginning at side of point, work

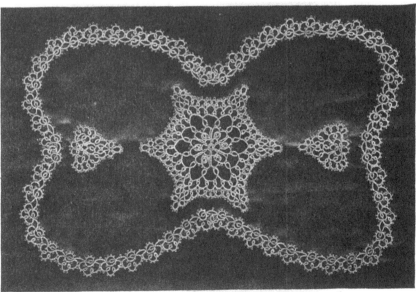

FIG. 88. DESIGN FOR SERVING TRAY. SEE PAGE 36

row of scallops around point of 2 sets 4-4 sts, a p of 3 beads, 2 sets 4-4 sts, join and repeat. On front side at top of purse work loop extending across two scallops, the ends of which are joined to cord, for convenience in opening purse.

CROCHET CORDS.—With hook join to ivory ring. Chain 50 sts, join to one side of purse at beginning of point. Ch 50, join to ring, ch 50, with hook draw the ch from back side of purse through the small space left between first and second scallops, of the row worked all around top of purse. With the hook join to the corresponding connection on front side of purse. Work a few sts, then draw this short ch and thread back through same space as entered and continue ch to ring. Repeat until all the spaces across purse are used and join last ch to extreme side of purse, as in beginning. There should be 7 sets of cords to ring, the last one ending at ring. Fill remainder of ring with double crochet and sew ends securely.

Figure 88. Tatting for Serving Tray. — Made with No. 30 crochet cotton.

CENTRAL MEDALLION. — With continuous thread. *Central ring*—7 d s, p, 7 d s, next r, ch, p, 2 p 3 d s between (bet), join p of r, p, 2 p 3 d s bet, fasten at base of r.

1st row—Leave ⅛ inch, r 3 d s, join base of central r, 3 d s; ch 2 p 3 d s bet, repeat, join rs at ps and top of r, and last at base of rs.

2d row—Ch 12 d s, 4 p 3 d s bet; double r, inside 7 d s, p, 7 d s; outside, ch 7 d s, join nearest p of 1st row, 2 d s, join p of r, 2 d s, join p of 1st row, 7 d s, join base of r. Ch 4 p 3 d s bet, 12 d s, join base of r in 1st row, repeat, joining chs of 12 d s to last ps of chs before p before the last chs. Cut threads and sew on the under side.

3d row—R, 9 d s, join 1st p after ch of 12 d s; 3 d s, join next p, 9 d s, close; ch 5 d s, p, 2 d s, p, 7 d s, p, 2 d s, p, 7 d s, p, 2 d s, p, 5 d s; r 9 d s, join 2d p after double r, 3 d s, join 3d p, 9 d s, close; ch 5 d s, p, 2 d s, p, 7 d s, p, 2 d s, p, 5 d s. Repeat rs and chs.

4th row—Rs all of 4 d s, join, 3 d s, join, 4 d s; each joined to a pair of ps of the last row. Chs, all of 3 or 5 p, 2 d s bet; 3 p over rs, 5 p over chs.

5th row—R 5 d s, join at the point, 2d ch of 5 p, join mid-p, 5 d s; ch 3 p 2 d s bet; r 4 d s join last p same ch, 2 d s, join next p, 4 d s; ch 3 p 2 d s bet, r 3 d s, join last p same ch, 2 d s join next p, 3 d s; ch 2 p 2 d s bet; r 3 d s

join mid-p next ch, 3 d s; ch 2 p 2 d s bet; r 3 d s, join last p of same ch, 2 d s, join next p, 3 d s; ch 3 p 2 d s bet; r 4 d s, join last p same ch, 2 d s, join 1st p next ch, 4 d s; ch 3 p 2 d s bet; r 5 d s, join mid-p of next ch, 5 d s; ch, 4 p 2 d s bet, 4 d s; r, 9 d s, join last p of ch, 2 p 3 d s between, 3 d s; ch 5 d s.

Clover leaf (c l) for the point—R, 5 d s, join last p, 3 d s, 3 p 2 d s bet, 3 d s, p, 5 d s; centre r, 5 d s, join last r, 5 d s, 5 p 2 d s bet, 5 d s, p, 5 d s. Third r of c l as first. Ch 5 d s; r 3 d s, join r, 3 d s, join same r, 3 d s, join last row, 9 d s; ch 4 d s, join p of c l, 3 p 2 d s bet. Repeat, making six points around.

MEDALLION FOR ENDS. — Make a star for the centre of 5 r, joined in p of first r, and 5 ch around them. Rs, 5 d s, p, 5 d s. Chs 3 p 3 d s bet.

2d row—Continue from first row,—ch 7 d s, 3 p 3 d s bet; r 7 d s, join mid-p in first row, 7 d s; ch 3 p 3 d s bet, 7 d s. Repeat twice, join 7 d s to 7 d s before.

3d row—Ch 7 d s, join last p; ch 3 d s, 3 p 2 d s bet; r 3 d s, join p of 2d row, 3 d s; ch 3 p 2 d s bet; repeat r and ch once. All rs join ps of last row. R 4 d s, join, 4 d s; ch 4 p 2 d s bet; repeat r and ch once; r 7 d s, join, 7 d s; ch 4 p 2 d s bet, 4 d s; r, 9 d s, join, 2 p 3 d s bet; ch 5 d s. Make a c l as in the central medallion and repeat rs and chs on the other side of the medallion.

EDGING. — R 7 d s, p, 7 d s; ch 4 p 3 d s bet, join p of r, 4 p 3 d s bet, join base of r; ch 5 d s, 4 p 3 d s bet; r 5 d s, join 2d p, 5 d s; ch 3 p 3 d s bet; r, join next p; ch 4 p 3 d s bet, 5 d s; turn, ch 7 d s, p, 7 d s. There are 56 scallops, 14 in each division.

FIG. 89. TATTED BAG. SEE PAGE 36

Figure 89. Bag.—Use No. 10 crochet cotton or silk.

SMALL MEDALLIONS. — R, 3 p 2 d s between (bet); very close, r 13 p 2 d s bet; push small r inside of large one, join at base; ch 4 d s. Repeat thrice, join and close. Join shuttle thread to 2d p of large r, make around it six r of 3 p 2 d s bet. Make two such medallions; then two more, the same, except that on three sides there are but 5 outer rs, the centre one of 9 p 2 d s bet. The centre medallion is the same, except there is a double r in place of large single r, of 13 p 2 d s bet, around which make 5 rs, 9 p 2 d s bet. The end medallions are placed squarely, the others diagonally.

To fill between medallions and straighten the work,

FIG. 90. DOILY WITH CORONATION CORD. SEE PAGE 37

Clover leaves (c l) of 5 d s, 5 p 2 d s bet, 5 d s, joined together; and to the cord by mid-p of the central r.

5th row—R 6 d s, 5 p 3 d s bet, 6 d s; ch 4 d s, 5 p 3 d s bet, 4 d s; join 2 r to each c l, and the mid-p of ch to the cord as before, making the *6th row*.

FIG. 90½. CORONATION CORD, FULL SIZE, USED IN DOILY FIG. 90

7th row—C ls of 6 d s, 7 p 3 d s bet, 6 d s, joined together and to the cord as before.

8th row—R 6 d s, 5 p 3 d s bet, 6 d s; ch 4 d s, 5 p 3 d s bet, 4 d s; join the rs together by the 1st ps; join two to each c l; and join chs to the cord, making the *9th row*.

10th row—C ls of 6 d s, 7 p 3 d s bet, 6 d s; join to the cord, and together by twos as shown in the cut.

Figure 91. Beaded Bag. (See Detail, Fig. 91½.)

Materials.— About 5 bunches turquoise opaque seed beads, 7 bunches white opaque seed beads, and Nos. 5 and 50 crochet cotton, No. 5 being used for padding chains in the braids. String many beads (b) of each color on separate balls, and a third of the two colors, alternately, six each. Begin with the row of rs for the drawing cord, and work downward.

1st row—Using the thread with white b as the upper one, make a

there is a row of chs of 7 p 2 d s bet; small rs of 3 p 2 d s bet; and large rs of 13 p 2 d s bet. Working down, join centre medallion, r at right of centre, 3d p. Ch, small r; ch, small r; large r join with long ps as shown in the cut; small r, ch, small r join large r of medallion, ch, small r, large r join by long ps, small r, ch, small r join, ch, small r join, ch, small r. Turn, ch, join mid-p of last ch, repeat chs to the top, joining mid-p centre r of centre figure. At the top turn and repeat first chs and rs to centre. Make ten rows like that, of chs only. At the end make 5 chs of 3 p, and 4 small rs joined to ends of medallion row. Finish the top with a row of chs, 7 p 2 d s bet, joined to centre ps of top chs; and rs, 3 p 2 d s bet. At the bottom make two rows of chs of 11 p 2 d s bet; the first, joining every other ch, the last, the chs left between; these rows join the sides of bag together.

Figure 90. Doily. *Materials.*—Three yards coronation cord (see Fig. 90½) and No. 24 spool cotton.

CENTRE RING.—10 l p 2 d s between (bet).

1st row—Of 10 alternate rs and chs, rings joined to the centre r. R 3 p 2 d s bet; ch 4 d s, 5 p 2 d s bet, 4 d s.

2d row— Repeat the first row, but with 15 rs and chs. Join rs to mid-p of chs of the first row, except every third r join ps of two adjoining chs; and join a narrow section of the cord to mid-p of each ch, forming the third row.

4th row—

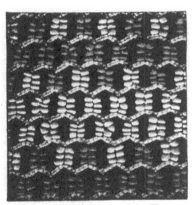

FIG. 91½. DETAIL OF BAG FIG. 91

FIG. 91. BAG IN BEADED TATTING. SEE DETAIL NO. 91½, AND PAGE 37

37

FIG. 92. NECKLACE IN BEADED TATTING. SEE DETAIL
FIG. 93, AND PAGE 38

r of 10 d s, p, 10 d s; ch 3 d s, p with 6 b, 3 d s.
Make 48 r, join first r, close.

2d row—Join, first b p; ch 3 d s, p with 6 b, 3 d s,
join next p and repeat. *3d row*—Like 2d. *4th row*—
Use the thread with mixed b, making the blue and
white ps alternately. *5th row*—Blue b. *6th row*—
Mixed b. *7th and 8th rows*—White. *9th row*—Mixed.
10th to 13th rows—Blue. *14th row*—Mixed. *15th and
16th rows*—White. *17th row*—Mixed. *18th row*—
Blue. *19th row*—Mixed. *20th to 22d rows*—White.

23d row—White. This row reaches only half way
and contains 23 ps.

24th row—Mixed. Join threads into first p of last
row and make 22 ps. *25th row*—Blue, 21 ps. *26th
row*—Blue, 20 ps. *27th row*—Mixed, 19 ps. *28th row*
—White, 18 ps. *29th row*—White, 17 ps. Finish the
other half in the same way.

Tie the thread into the top of the p in the 22d row,
which is exactly at the side of the bag and ch 6 d s;
make a long beaded p, using a piece of cardboard 2¾
inches long as a measure and twist the thread so that
the beaded thread will twist when the p is made;
ch 3 d s, and join through the top of the two succes-
sive ps in the 23d row. Repeat till there are 8 long
twisted ps, then make 3 d s, p, 3 d s in the chs across
the bottom, joining the two sides together.

Now returning to the top, make a row like the first
one joining the rs to those in the first row, with white
b ps. *2d row*—Blue b. Join into top of a white p in
last row and ch 5 d s, p, with 5 b, 5 d s, join to next p,
p with 5 b over joining; repeat to end of row. Fasten
all ends on back of work with No. 100 thread.

The cord is the d ch (see Fig. 110) made with 3
strands of padding cotton No. 5 on the shuttle, and
two strands of the No. 50 with blue beads on the
upper, and white ones on the lower thread. Holding
the three threads between left thumb and finger with
the heavy thread between the other two, pass the

upper and lower threads around the fingers, being
careful that they do not cross, but lie a little apart.

Now take the middle shuttle in the right hand,
and with the thumb and finger slip the lower thread
off the fingers, without loosening the left thumb and
finger, and draw it back under the left thumb where
it is held out of the way while an ordinary d s is
made with the upper thread. Now slip the under
thread back over the fingers and make a d s with it.
Make the last half of this d s, as ordinarily made,
first and draw it tight with the right hand, then make
the first part of the stitch. Continue making d s,
first with the upper and then the lower thread, till
the cord is about a foot long, then make ps of 3 b
each, separated by 5 d s on either side, until you have
made another foot, then another foot plain. Make
two of these cords, double the beaded part in the
centre and tie with loops. Also tie a knot in the
doubled cord below the beaded part. Draw the ends
of one cord through the upper row of rings in the
bag; the other through the lower row, and join the
ends. The bag may be lined or used unlined, as
desired.

Figure 92. Beaded Necklace. (See Detail, Fig.
93.) *Materials.*—One bunch No. o gold and one
bunch No. o bronze beads, one string No. o pearl
beads, two brilliants, clasp, and No. 40 crochet cotton.

String beads on ball thread in following order:
1 bronze (b), 1 gold (g), 4 b, 1 g, 1 pearl (p), 1 g,
4 b, 1 g, 2 b, 1 g, 6 b, 1 g, 3 b; this is for one section
of necklace. Repeat for each section, then add 1 b,
1 g, 4 b, 1 g, 1 p, 1 g, 4 b, 1 g, 1 b. The necklace is
begun and ended with the long loop, making 30 long
loops, a pendant in front, and 30 scallops at top of
necklace.

Push beads along on thread and fill shuttle from
same ball. Begin work as described in Fig. 94. *Long
loops*—Work 15 d s, bringing the sts close to the knot;
draw thread through sts to the knot; make a beaded
picot by slipping first three beads (1 b, 1 g, 1 b)
close to sts already made, continue with 5 d s, then
a beaded picot of 9 beads, having the p bead in the
centre; work 5 d s; another beaded picot like first
one; 12 d s, draw
shuttle thread
close through
whole ch and
form long loop
of this chain by
crossing it 2 d s
from the begin-
ning, ball thread
under, shuttle
thread over the
ch. Continue
with 3 d s, a
beaded picot of
1 b; repeat
twice, 3 d s, pi-
cot, 6 d s, a bead-
ed picot of 3
beads (1 b, 1 g,
1 b), 6 d s and
form loop as be-
fore, crossing at
beginning of ch.

FIG. 93. DETAIL OF NECKLACE
FIG. 92. FULL SIZE

To make the scallop over last loop, continue from crossing, 4 d s, beaded picot of 1 b 3 d s, another b picot, 3 d s, a beaded picot of 3 beads as before; repeat first half of scallop, carry this ch over top of last loop, and join to the plain picot of that loop. This completes one section. At one end of necklace sew one section of the clasp in place, then with same thread fasten 1 g bead, 1 p, and 1 g in open space in small loop; repeat in each loop, and sew the other section of clasp in place at last end.

To make pendant: At centre front sew a brilliant in centre long loop, from one side of loop string b and g beads alternately to a little below the beaded picot of that loop, then a p bead, 1 g, 1 b, 1 g, pass thread through another brilliant, 1 g, 1 b, 1 g, 1 p, 1 b, 1 g, 1 b, pass back through the pearl, 1 g, 1 b, 1 g, pass through last brilliant and repeat on the other side.

FIG. 94. NECKLACE IN BEADED TATTING. SEE DETAIL FIG. 95, AND PAGE 39

Figure 94. Tatted Necklace. (See Detail, Fig. 95.) —It is hard to realize that this handsome necklace is made with the tatting shuttle. The materials required are No. 40 crochet cotton, 1 bunch No. 6 steel beads, 1 bunch jet beads a little larger, 1 string No. 2 pearl beads, and a clasp.

String a quantity of beads (b) on ball thread: 1 black (b) to two steel (s).

Fill shuttle from same ball, slipping b back on ball. Ch 2 d s, then 4 sets 4-4 sts (see Explanations on page 3). Work 1 d s, p, 1 d s; repeat the four sets of sts, 1 d s, draw shuttle thread close, form a loop of this ch of sts by crossing ch 1 d s from beginning, shuttle thread over, and ball thread under ch, work 1 d s, slip the b along, work one set of 4-4 sts, make a b p, using 1 b between 2 s. Work one set of 5-5 sts, another b p, another set of 5 sts, another b p, and a set of five sts, 1 d s. Carry this ch around side of the loop first made and join to p at end of loop. Make next loop as first, except 1 d s before half sts instead of two in beginning, and join by crossing the ch close to first loop, make b ch as before.

Continue to length required, then make b ch of sts as before, carry around other side of loop last made and join between that loop and next one back. Work back whole length of necklace, joining each b ch between loops. Have an even number of loops in the necklace. Fasten off ends at first end of work and sew the clasp for fastening to each end.

With needle and cotton, same as used, sew through whole length of necklace, in open space in each loop, 1 pearl bead between 2 s, passing thread through work between loops.

The pendants are fastened one in centre of front and one on each side of centre three loops from centre. These are made in same way, making two long loops, one to fit inside the other, with b p on the side and at the bottom, using more b with a pearl bead in centre of string. For side pendants make one long loop, then string s, b, and pearl beads in any fancy shape and hang in centre of each tatted loop.

Figure 96. Candle-Shade. — Use one ball No. 50 crochet cotton and gold beads.

TRIANGLE. — Clover leaf; r, 5 p 4 d s between (bet); repeat the r twice, drawing close, and joining the r before, at ps. Ch, 7 d s, p, 7 d s. Repeat c l and ch twice, joining chs to p of the first ch, and c ls to the upper c l, as shown in the cut.

WHEEL. — Centre r, 10 long p, 2 d s bet. Make the long ps over a cardboard strip ⅞ inch wide, to make evenly. Make circle of 10 r. * R 8 d s, p, 8 d s, ch 2 d s, p, 2 d s, p, 2 d s, join p of centre r, 2 d s, p, 2 d s, p, 2 d s, join p of r, ch, 4 d s. Repeat from * 9 times, joining ps of centre r. Around this circle; after joining, turn; * ch 5 d s, join p of last r, ch 7 p 2 d s bet, join p of same r, ch 5 d s. Repeat from * around circle, joining 2 r to the triangle, as shown in the cut.

EDGING.—* R 6 d s, p, 6 d s; ch 3 p 2 d s bet, join p of r. Repeat from *

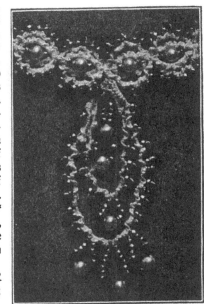

FIG. 95. DETAIL OF NECKLACE
FIG. 94. FULL SIZE

39

FIG. 96. CANDLE SHADE. SEE PAGE 39

around the panel, joining c ls of the triangle, as shown in the cut, and to two side r of the wheel. At the next, add another r between two r of the edging, joined by the p to the wheel. *

Make three r, add another r and join the next r of the wheel. Repeat from * twice, then continue as before, around the panel.

Outside row—String 75 gold beads, then fill the shuttle, pushing the beads back on the thread. Ch 2 d s, slide one bead close to the ds, make in all, four times, 2 d s with one bead following; join base of r. Use the beads only at the top and bottom, omitting them on the rings which join the panels. Make five of the panels.

Figure 97. Baby Bonnet. — Two balls of crochet silk will be needed.

WHEELS. — R 2 d s, 12 p 2 d s between (bet), 2 d s; r 3 d s, p, 3 d s, join a p of r, 3 d s, p, 3 d s. Turn, leave a short thread; r 6 d s, p, 6 d s, 3 p 2 d s bet, 6 d s, p, 6 d s. Repeat until there are 12 r of each size, the smaller joined to the centre r, the larger joined together.

First row of six wheels—Join wheels while making by two r of each. Fill the space between three free r with r of 5 d s, p, 5 d s, join 1st r, 5 d s, p, 5 d s, join 2d r, 5 d s, p, 5 d s, join 3d r, close. Fill the larger space between wheels with a four-r figure of 6 d s, p, 6 d s, join, 6 d s, p, 6 d s.

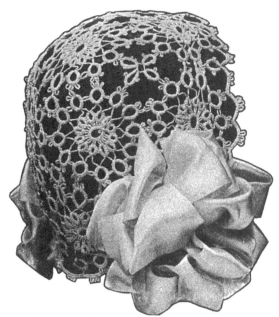

FIG. 97. BABY BONNET. SEE PAGE 40

Edging of rs and chs. — R 6 d s, p, 6 d s, join the joining of the first and second wheels, 6 d s, p, 6 d s. Ch 6 d s, 3 p 3 d s bet, 6 d s, join mid-p of next r. Repeat ch and r at next joining.

Figure 98. Motif. — Made of crochet cotton No. 50 or 60. Make r 3 d s, p, 3 d s, small p, 3 d s, p, 2 d s, p, 3 d s; turn, shuttle thread under, ball thread over, keep side of r with 1 p uppermost; ch 5 d s, 5 p, 2 d s between (bet), 5 d s, join small p of r. Repeat. Make 26 figures, those adjoining turned in opposite directions. Join the 23d scallop to the first by mid-ps. At the top make chs, only on the upper sides, of three rs.

CENTRE INSERTION. — Begin with a p; ch 3 d s; join 2d p of 4th ch after centre one at the top, and also 4th p of the ch opposite, 2 p 3 d s bet, join, at right side, 1st p of next inner ch, 3 d s, p, 3 d s; join p at beginning. Reverse, 3 d s, p, 3 d s, join mid-p of next left ch, 3 d s, p, 3 d s, join p of first ch. Reverse, ch 3 d s, join p of next ch, 3 d s, p, 3 d s, join mid-p of same ch on right side, 2 p 3 d s bet, join p of 2d ch. Repeat, make 10 chs, joining as shown in the cut.

Figure 100. Candle-Shade. — Made of dark red crochet cotton and steel beads. Do not break the thread from the ball.

Upper row—* Clover leaf (c l), rs 4 d s, 7 p, 2 d s between (bet), 4 d s, join leaves together; ch 4 d s, 3 p 4 d s bet, 4 d s, join to 4th p in c l, repeat ch, join next r of c l, ch 5 d s and repeat from *. Make 12 c l, join last ch to first ch, and last c l to base of first.

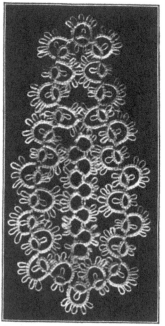

FIG. 98. TATTED MOTIF. SEE PAGE 40

Ch, 5 d s, join mid-p of last c l; ch 4 d s, join 1st p of last ch; ch 4 d s, p, 4 d s, join mid-p of first r; ch 4 d s, 3 p 4 d s bet, 4 d s, join base of next c l. Repeat.

SPIDER-WEBS. — Make centre r of 14 l ps 2 d s bet, tie. Make the long p over a strip of cardboard for evenness. R 4 d s, join a l p, 4 d s, leave a short thread, join 2d p of 2d ch of c l, r 4 d s, join next l p, 4 d s; join thread to 3d p in first ch of next c l. r, 4 d s, join l p, 4 d s; join ch of second c l. Leaving a short thread between, continue around the spider-web.

WHEEL. — Centre r; string 7 beads, make a r of 14 d s, alternately, 1 d s, bead, 1 d s, p, close. Make a double row of small r 4 d s, join, 4 d s, join two small r in one p of centre r; large r, joined together, of 4 d s, 3 p 2 d s bet, join spider-web, 3 p 2 d s bet, 4 d s. Leave a short thread between the large and small r, and join six upper r to the spider-web.

EDGE.—String 270 beads on the ball thread, r 4 d s, join between two r of the spider-web 4 d s, ch, 4 d s, bead, 4 beads 2 d s bet, 4 d s; r 4 d s, join r of the wheel 4 d s. Alternate rs and chs,—joining rs to the wheel or spider-web,—all around the shade.

Figure 101. Baby Bonnet. (See detail, Fig. 99.)— Use No. 50 crochet cotton. Begin the crown with a r of 12 p 2 d s between (bet); leave a short thread; r 4 d s, join 1st p of centre r, ·4 d s; turn, leave short thread, r 4 d s, 3 p 8 d s bet, 4 d s, continue around centre r. Next row of chs; 6 p 2 d s bet, join large rs. A double row of alternate large and small r, the small ones joined to 2d and 5th ps of chs. R 4 d s, join, 4 d s, leave a short thread, r 4 d s, 3 p 8 d s bet, 4 d s, join large r together.

Next row chs of 7 p 2 d s bet joined to the last row. This completes the crown.

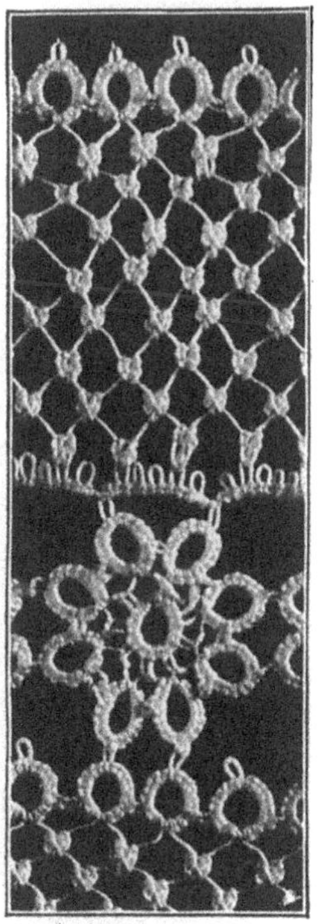

Next row of small rings; r 2 d s, join 2d p of ch, 2 d s; leave thread for a scallop; repeat ring, join 6th p of ch; repeat around. The next row join rs to thread scallop, make 5 rows thus. A row of small wheels. Centre r, 8 p 2 d s bet; r 3 d s, 3 p 6 d s bet, 3 d s, join p of centre r; make 8 r; joined together, and joined to centre, the last two r joining the row before. Join wheels by two side r, and at the back closer together in joining last row, to draw the bonnet in. *Next row*—Ch, 5 p 2 d s between ps of a wheel, ch 7 p 2 d s between, between wheels. The next 6 rows repeat the 5 rows before the wheels. At the back skip several small r to shape the bonnet to the head. The next row is double; of the small rs, and larger ones of 3 d s, 3 p

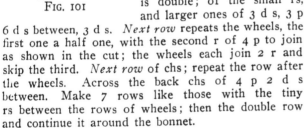

FIG. 99. DETAIL OF FIG. 101

6 d s between, 3 d s. *Next row* repeats the wheels, the first one a half one, with the second r of 4 p to join as shown in the cut; the wheels each join 2 r and skip the third. *Next row* of chs; repeat the row after the wheels. Across the back chs of 4 p 2 d s between. Make 7 rows like those with the tiny rs between the rows of wheels; then the double row and continue it around the bonnet.

Figure 102. Doily. (See detail, Fig. 103.) — Use No. 16 spool cotton, or No. 30 crochet cotton.

Daisy—Centre r, 4 d s, 8 p 4 d s between (bet), 4 d s; around it, r 5 p 4 d s bet, join p of centre r; leave very short thread, r 3 p 4 d s bet joined to last r. and p of centre r; make four large and four small r, joined. Join the daisies by 2 p of the larger rs. and 1 p of the smaller rs of the adjoining daisies, of which there are 24. The two inner rows are of chs. 4 d s, p, 4 d s, joined as in the cut. The inner row is of 3 d s, p, 3 d s. The outside row. r 4 d s, join p of daisy, 4 d s; ch, 2 p 4 d s bet. The linen may be

rolled or stitched; and buttonholed as the tatting is joined.

Figure 104. Handkerchief Border in Tatted Net. —Use No. 100 crochet cotton. The

FIG. 100. BEADED CANDLE SHADE. SEE PAGE 40

first and last rows are of blue cotton, the net of white.

1st row—Join while making; with a fine crochet-hook, loop thread through the hem, and pass shuttle through the loop. Ch 2 sets 4-4 sts, picot, 2 sets 4-4 sts, join ¼ inch apart; around points of corners, ch 2 sets 4-4 sts, picot, 1 set 4-4 sts, picot, 2 sets 4-4 sts.

2d row—With shuttle thread only; ring 4 d s, join picot, 4 d s; leave thread ⅜ inch, repeat ring, join next picot; join 2 rings to each picot of corner scallops. Repeat 2d row thrice, join thread between rings; at corners, join 2 rings to centre thread.

6th row—5 picots 2 d s between, join thread of last row.

Figure 105. Tatted Yoke. — Use crochet cotton No. 50.

Large squares—Centre r, 4 p 4 d s between (bet). Ch 6 d s; r 4 d s, 7 p 2 d s bet, 4 d s; repeat twice, joining for clover leaf; ch 6 d s, join p of centre r. Repeat 3 times. Make and join 7 squares. On each side of the squares add a double row of r 4 d s, p, 6 d s, p, 6 d s, p, 4 d s. Add a row to each, of small squares of 4 r, of 3 p 6 d s bet, the rs joined together, the squares at the points together, and to the double row before. Then to the outside, add 1 double row.

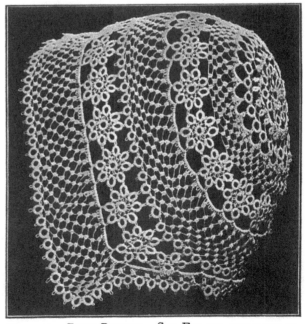

FIG. 101. BABY BONNET. SEE FIG. 99, AND PAGE 41

To the inside, after the small squares, add one double row, of rs 4 d s, 3 p 6 bet, 4 d s, and smaller rs, inside, of 6 d s, p, 6 d s. Then the double edging row, rs 6 d s, p, 6 d s;—3 p 4 d s bet,—and 4 d s, 10 p 2 d s bet, 4 d s, but the last 11 outside r should be only of 3 p 4 d s bet, omitting the larger rs. Increase or decrease the length of rows to fit the shoulder, as shown in the cut. Make a like section for the other side, and join the two by a crosspiece, as shown in the cut. Beginning at a shoulder, make a double row around the yoke to the top of the other shoulder. The back may be either of muslin, a narrow band of the tatting, or a duplicate of the front. The two upper rows form a beading for ribbon.

Figure 106. Collar. (See detail Fig. 107.)—Crochet cotton No. 10 is used.

MEDALLION.—R 3 p 2 d s between; ch 3 d s; r 7 p 2 d s between (bet); ch 3 d s; repeat small r, ch, large r, ch; join and sew ends underneath. This forms the centre figure. Join in 2 p of adjoining rs; * ch 12 d s, join ps of next two rs; ch 18 d s, join; repeat once, from *. Make a similar ch row of 16 and 22 d s.

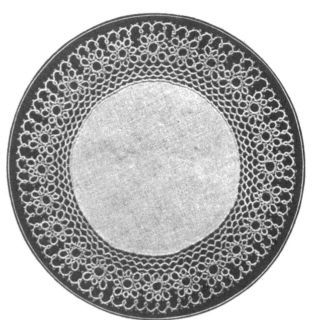

FIG. 102. DOILY. SEE DETAIL FIG. 103, AND PAGE 41

The third ch row is of 6 p 3 d s bet; and 8 p 3 d s bet. The row of small r; over the smaller ch has 6 r, 3 p 2 d s between, over the larger, 8 r, all joined to ps of the last row.

The last 4 rows may be slip-stitched, between them, to avoid ends. Join medallions together by mid-ps of two side r, in making or sewing afterwards.

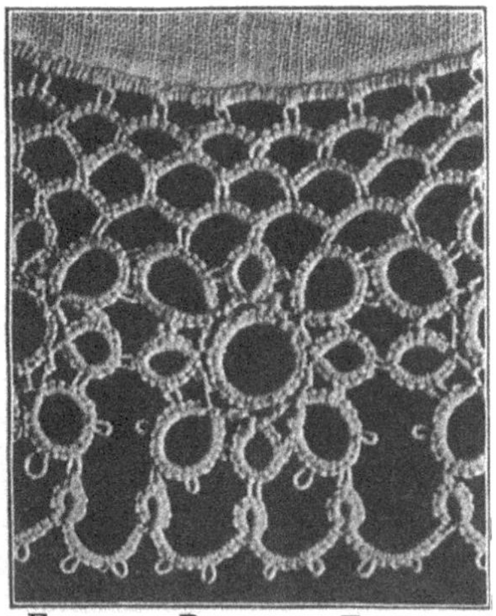

FIG. 103. DETAIL OF FIG. 102.

BORDER AROUND MEDALLIONS.—Keep all parts of the collar right side up. Join the first front medallion between the side and lower chs of rs, by a picot each, of 2 r; ch 11 d s p, join 3d r; ch 18 d s p, join 3d r; ch 11 d s p, join between scallops. Ch 7 d s turn, r 3 p 2 d s bet, joined to the second r; the joining of the medallions; and the next r; ch 7 d s. Repeat around. At the left front, turn; ch 4 p 3 d s between, join p of row before; ch 6 p 3 d s bet, join; ch 4 p 3 d s bet, join; ch 7 d s, turn; r 3 p 2 d s bet, turn in opposite direction from r above; ch 7 d s, close.

Begin at the right front, join shuttle thread only, to 1st p on last ch, on this ch work three r, 7 p 2 d s bet, join ps, small r 3 p 2 d s bet, join between chs; 5 r 7 p 2 d s bet, join ps; repeat small r, 2 large r, small r. Slip-stitch thread to mid-p of small r and join p of r of last row; carry thread to next p of ch, make small r join mid-p to joinings of last two r. Except at the front ends, make but 1 small and 2 large r to the side chs of each scallop. Continue around. Make a figure like the medallion centre, but with three small r, the large one upper; join the 3 r as shown in the cut.

BORDER AROUND THE NECK.—Join continuous thread between 4th and 5th r of side scallop, left front. Ch 8 d s, join 1st r on next scallop, ch 8 d s; r 3 p 2 d s bet; turn, make two ch over the last two of 5 p 2 d s bet; close. Repeat on the right front. Join thread in p of last small r, join p of 3d r on medallion; ch 8 d s, join 4th r medallion; ch 8 d s; r 3 p 2 d s bet; ch 8 d s, join large r of connecting figure; ch 8 d s, join 2d r; ch 8 d s, join 2d r; ch 8 d s; r 3 p 2 d s bet; ch 8 d s join large r; repeat. At the end turn; join mid-p of small r; chs of 3 p 2 d s between, joined between chs of last row.

For the last row around neck; join at the joining of the two end scallops and the small r; ch 3 p 2 d s bet; r 3 p 2 d s bet; ch 3 p 2 d s bet, join mid-p of last ch. Repeat rs and chs around the neck. Fasten all ends with fine thread; and press the collar under a damp cloth.

Figure 108. Bag. (See detail, Fig. 109.)—Use crochet cotton No. 10.

MEDALLIONS.—With continuous thread make the medallions (med) first. R 3 p 2 d s between (bet), ch 9 d s. Make 6 r and 6 ch, to form a circle; ch 13 d s, 6 times, join base of rs. Ch 5 p 3 d s bet, 6 times, join ch at base of rs. On these chs work 5 r, 3 p 2 d s bet, join 1st r between chs. This forms one of the 4 smaller med. To make the large centre one, add ch 28

FIG. 104. HANDKERCHIEF BORDER IN TATTED NET. SEE PAGE 41

d s, join between scallops. Ch 11 p 3 d s bet, around each scallop, and on each ch work 10 r. The first and last on each scallop 3 p 1 d s bet, and the other s the large one, s on each side, as seen in the cut.

BACKGROUND.—To fill in around these med, join between 2d and 3d rs of centre scallop of large med and ch 7 d s. R 3 p 2 d s bet; join centre p between 3d and 4th rs of the next scallop, ch 13 d s, r 11 p 2 d s bet; join 4th p in r, to centre p of 5th r in same scallop, and 8th p of same r to centre p of 2d r in opposite scallop on the smaller med. Ch 13 d s, r 3 p, join between 2d and 3d rs in next scallop. Repeat ch r, ch, and large r, join 4th p to centre p in 4th r of scallop. Cut and tie threads. Begin at other side of large med and repeat directions. After last large r, turn, ch 5 d s, 1 p, 5 d s, r 3 p 2 d s bet, join centre p at base of large r, ch 6 p 2 d s bet, r 3 p 2 d s bet, join at base of small r in previous

row in which to run the cord and on which are the figures to finish the top of the bag. To make the sides of the bag even at side of small med, join threads at base of small r joined to a large r and alternate rs and chs to base of large r on the other side of small med. This completes one side of the bag, the sides may be tatted or sewed together. The med above and below the centre are sewed on.

TATTED CORD.—Wind several yards of thread double, to make a heavy cord; join to a figure like those at bottom of bag. Ch 5 d s, sm p, 5 d s. Continue to the desired length, run through the top of the bag, join another figure, turn, ch 4 d s join p on ch, ch 4 d s, join; continue the length of the ch. Do not draw the shuttle thread too tight, to keep the ch straight.

Figure 111. Beaded Cords and Trimmings.

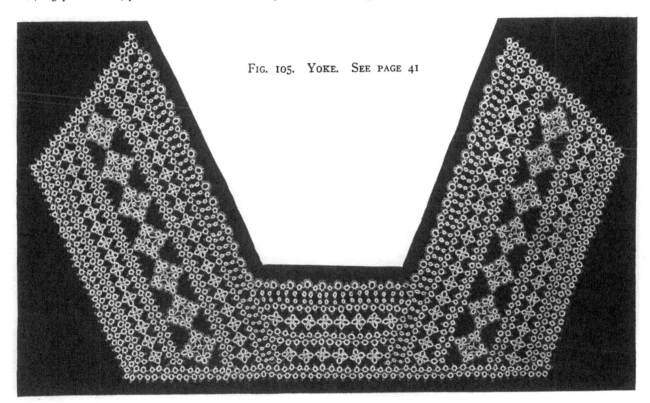

FIG. 105. YOKE. SEE PAGE 41

row. Continue chs and rs until large med is reached. Join ch to centre p of the 4th r in scallop, ch 6 p 2 d s bet, join centre p of 7th r in scallop. Continue rs and chs to last large r. Turn, ch 5 d s, 1 p 5 d s, and repeat rs and chs. Make 8 rows in all. Then without turning work, ch 5 d s, p, 5 d s; r 3 p 2 d s between.

MEDALLIONS ON BASE, TOP AND ENDS OF CORDS.— Turn, ch 6 p 2 d s between, join centre p to centre p of previous row, r 3 p 2 d s bet, ch 7 d s, join 1st p of r, ch 9 d s, join 3d p in r, ch 7 d s, join at base of r, ch 3 p 3 d s bet, join between chs, ch 4 p 3 d s between, join, ch 3 p 3 d s bet, join. On 1st and 3d ch make 3 r, 3 p 2 d s bet; on centre ch make 4 r, 3 p 2 d s bet, join threads at base of r, ch 6 p 2 d s bet, r 3 p 2 d s bet, repeat chs and rs and on every 3d r make this figure as directed. This finishes the bottom of the bag. Make upper part of bag with 15 rows of chs and small rs. Reverse the

A Three strands of padding cord (p c) (No. 3 crochet cotton) on the shuttle, and two balls of No. 50 crochet cotton are used, with blue seed beads on one, white ones on the other. Tie the 3 threads together, the heavy thread in the middle; hold the knot with left thumb and finger. Pass the lighter threads around the left fingers a little apart. Ch 1 d s with the upper thread, turn the work *toward* you, half way around; ch 1 d s, with the lower thread, turn back *from* you; ch 1 d s, turn; ch 1 d s, turn, push up a bead closely, ch 1 d s. Have 2 d s on each side between beads.

B Same as A, but with a p of three beads.

C With two strands of p c, and blue and white beads (b) strung alternately. *1st row*—Chain 2 d s, p, turn, 2 d s, b, turn, 2 d s p, turn, 2 d s b, repeat. *2d row*—Join 1st p, using two strands of p c on shuttle and ch; ch 2 d s b, 2 d s b, 2 d s b, 2 d s; join the next p.

D *1st row*—Like B, but with 4 beads, on the lower side, in each p. In the second row, on the upper side, join the ps of beads; make the lower ps of 3 blue beads. White beads in the middle, blue on upper and lower sides.

E The middle row (made first) is of 5 d s; 6 blue b above, and 6 white b below. No padding in upper and lower rows; ch with No. 50 cotton, ps of three blue beads.

FIG. 106. ROUND COLLAR. SEE DETAIL FIG. 107, AND PAGE 42

upper side of the daisies. Six rows with r 4 d s, join, 4 d s; three rows with r 3 d s, join, 3 d s. BORDER.—*1st row*—Join thread between rs; ch 2 sets 4-4 sts, p, 2 sets, join next thread. *2d row*—Carry thread to p of 1st scallop, repeat scallop, join next p, ch 7 p 3 d s bet, join p of 2d scallop. *3d and 4th rows*—As the 3 rows before the border; in 3d row join 3 rs to 2d, 4th and 6th ps of large scallop, and by thread to p of small scallop. *5th row*—Ch, 5 ps 2 d s bet, join loops of thread. *6th row*—Ch 6 p 2 d s bet, join 3d p of scallops.

For the lining and finishing—Silk 9 x 12 inches, sewing silk and tassel to match, and 2 yards narrow white satin ribbon. Turn 2 inches of the lining at the top, stitch 3 rows, the upper 2 a shirring for the ribbon. Gather the bottom closely, pass the tassel loop through the daisy and gathering, and sew neatly together. Sew the lower edge of border to the silk; run in the ribbon and make loops at the sides. This dainty bag is lined with messaline silk of a delicate color.

Figure 112. Handkerchief Bag. — Made with No. 60 crochet cotton, mercerized. See page 3 for "sets of 4-4 stitches." Make 10 daisies of 8 petals each, thus: ch 4 d s, 5 sets 4-4 sts, p, 5 sets, 3 d s. Form first petal, crossing ch 1 d s from beginning, shuttle thread over, ball thread under ch. Make 7 more petals close together. Join last to first petal at base, tie, and sew ends closely. Join daisies together by one petal, and 9th to the 1st. The 10th is for the bottom of the bag. Work downward. *1st row*—With shuttle thread only; r 5 d s, join 1st of 3 petals of a daisy, 5 d s. Leave ½ inch of thread, repeat r, join next petal; repeat r, join 3d petal; repeat r, join the joining of two daisies. *2d and 3d rows*—As first row, join rs to thread between rs of row before. *4th row*—R 4 d s, join, 4 d s; narrow by joining every 3d r to 2 loops of thread. *5th to 8th rows*—As 2d and 3d rows. *9th row*—Repeat 4th row. *10th to 12th rows*—R 3 d s, join, 3 d s. Finish by sewing petals of the single daisy to two threads between rings, or three threads, as needed to narrow evenly. *Upper part of bag*—Repeat the first 4 rows, on the

FIG. 107. DETAIL OF COLLAR, FIG. 106

Figure 113. Insertions in Padded Tatting. — A requires 2 shuttles, and is of 2 rows; use 3 strands of padding. Make a row of double ch as the upper cord in Fig. 68. Ch 3 d s; r 6 d s, p, 6 d s; repeat r, 1 d s, then 6 d s on both sides. Repeat r, join p of last r, repeat r 1 d s, and continue.

B The lower design is made with two shuttles, and three strands of padding. Ch 5 d s, leave a little space, 4 d s, 3 p 4 d s between, join, with a fine crochet-hook, the little space left, drawing the upper thread back of the lower thread, through the ch under the heavy thread, and pass shuttle through the loop, drawing very tightly. Turn and repeat. Join rings by side ps.

Figure 114. Rose Spray.—This pretty hair ornament is made with white crochet cotton Nos. 20 and 60; milliner's fine covered wire and fine gold beads.

ROSES. — With s thread No. 20 make r of 30 p separated by 1½ d s, draw tightly to make r as small as possible. Sl st thread to 1st p, string 100 beads on ball thread and join shuttle thread.

1st row of petals—* Two d s, 2 p separated by 1 d s, 1 d s, slip a bead (b) close to last st; 1 d s, p, 1 d s, bead, 1 d s, p, 1 d s, p, 1 d s, p, 2 d s *. Join this ch to next p on r, making first petal; make six around r. Join shuttle thread to 4th p from last joining, passing thread under and skipping 3 p between joining *. Repeat between *, join to next p on r and continue around ring.

2d row of petals—After sixth petal of 1st row, sl st thread to p at *left* of first petal, then work as in 1st row, * making ch of 2 d s, 3 p, 5 beaded p, with 1 p between, 3 p, 2 d s, join to 1st p on *right* side of first petal *. This forms first petal of 2d row. Pass thread under 1 p on r and join p at left of next petal of 1st row. Repeat between * and join as before. Continue around r to complete 2d row. There should now be 1 p between petals all around r, * sl st to 1st p, ch 2 d s, 4 p, 8 b p with

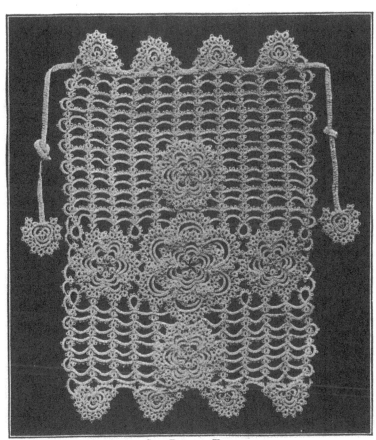

FIG. 108. BAG. SEE DETAIL FIG. 109, AND PAGE 42

FIG. 109. DETAIL OF BAG, FIG. 108

1 p between each, 4 p, 2 d s, join next p between petals, * repeat between *. Continue around r to complete 3d row. This brings the three rows of petals in direct line with each other from the centre.

CENTRE OF ROSE.—Make small crocheted ball (see directions for Fig. 19), stuff with cotton, leave 8 or 10 inches thread at close, cut 4 or 5 inches wire, pass one end through ball at finished end, double wire end, close, and wind neatly with end of cotton left on ball to cover end of wire.

Now pass the free end of wire downward through centre of rose, pulling about one-half of the ball through the ring in centre of rose, the lower half making the bulb and the upper half the rose centre, sew beads in upper half and sew ball to ring of rose on under side to hold in place.

BUDS. — First make crocheted ball as for rose, finishing it with wire stem, winding enough thread around wire end to resemble the bulb at base of a rosebud. Chain 4 d s, beaded p, plain p, alternating until there are 4 b p, 3 plain p, graded in length, the first and last being ⅛ inch, the centre one ¼ inch in length, 4 b p and 3 d s. Bring ends of ch together, pass shuttle thread over, ball thread under at point of ch, 1 d s from beginning. Draw shuttle thread close, work 2 d s to hold ch in form of petal. Make three more

45

petals, beginning each quite close to one preceding, 2 d s after close of fourth petal and join to beginning of first petal forming a tiny space in centre of the four

FIG. 110. CORONATION CORD, FULL SIZE, USED IN BAG, FIG. 116, PAGE 48

petals, pass wire attached to crocheted ball through this space, pull down closely, sew in place, also the petals around ball to complete rosebud. Make four more petals left spreading down from bud, sewing them at base of bud to hold in place.

LEAF CLUSTER.—Cut two pieces wire each 6 in. in length, and one piece 8 in. long. Cover these wires closely with double crochet with No. 60 cotton, leaving ½ in. wire at each end of the shorter pieces; and 1½ in. on the longer piece for stem.

TATTED EDGE OF LEAF.—Join threads at beginning of crochet covering, work 3 d s, 3 p separated by

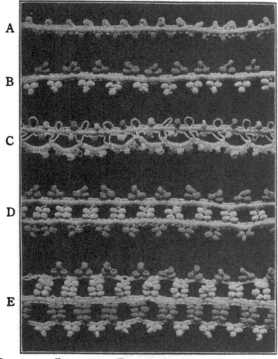

FIG. 111. CORDS AND TRIMMINGS IN BEADED TATTING. SEE PAGE 43

1 d s, 3 d s, join to third or fourth st from first joining. (This depends on how closely the crochet is done), repeat all around or the length of each covered wire. Bring the ends of each wire together at beginning of covering and wind to cover ends of threads.

TATTED CENTRE OF LEAVES.—String on shuttle thread 50 beads. Take thread between thumb and finger of left hand, slip 6 b up close before passing thread around hand. Work 2 d s, 3 b p with 1 p between, 2 d s, 1 p, 2 d s, 3 b p 1 p between, 2 d s, join, draw closely.

Carry thread upward through end of ring, slip as many beads as will fill open space in r, join to centre p of r. Make 4 r in this manner, each being made

close to the one preceding it. Increase number of beads in 2d and 3d r to 8, and in 4th r decrease to 6, as in 1st r. Sew ends of this ch of r to ends of wire leaves on under side, also the plain p on sides of r to the sides of the leaves.

Arrange the three sections in form of cluster of rose leaves. Wind wires together for stem. Group three roses, two buds, and leaf cluster prettily, and wind all stems together as compactly and smoothly as

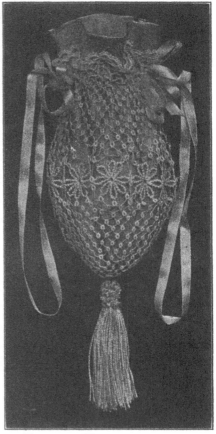

FIG. 112. HANDKERCHIEF BAG. SEE PAGE 44

possible. One or two long wire hairpins may be twisted among the stems to hold ornament in the hair, and the leaves made to cover pins.

Figure 115. Butterfly.—Use No. 20 crochet cotton. BODY IN CROCHET.—Ch 4, join, fill ch with 8 d. *2d row*—Two d in each st of 1st row. *3d and 4th rows*—Plain. *5th row*—Skip every 2d st. *6th row*—Two d in each st of last row, now stuff with cotton, part made for head. *7th and 8th rows*—Plain. Narrow off by skipping each fourth st until closed, stuff

FIG. 113. INSERTIONS IN PADDED TATTING. SEE PAGE 44

body when nearly closed. Body, including head, should be 1½ inches in length.

WINGS. — Use milliner's fine covered wire for foundation. For the larger wings cut wire 18 in., and for smaller wings, 12 in. in length. Make a sharp bend at centre of longer wire, which place a little below the head on crochet body, fasten temporarily while shaping on either side of body, bring ends of wire together, lap ⅓ in. under body about ½ in. lower than centre of wire. Make slight bend in centre of shorter wire, bring ends around to centre in long loops, lap as before, fasten to centre bend to form smaller wings. After fastening ends of both wires, bend them into proper shape for the outline of each pair of wings, then remove from body and leave ends free while covering wire, it will be found much easier. Cover wire of both pairs of wings very closely with No. 60 crochet cotton in d c.

TATTED EDGE. — Join threads about ½ in. from end of wire to crochet cover, 2 d s, 3 p separated by 1 d s, 2 d s, centre p longer than others, join to 4th st on wire from first joining. Continue around both pairs of wings.

Now make 8 tatted coils; wind thread a few times around shuttle, but do not disconnect.

FIG. 114. ROSE SPRAY IN BEADED TATTING FOR HAIR. SEE PAGE 45

FIG. 115. BUTTERFLY IN BEADED TATTING. SEE PAGE 46

Take doubled end of thread between thumb and forefinger of left hand, pass ball thread around left hand, hold firmly the doubled end while with shuttle thread work a few d s, then draw shuttle thread through tightly, and thus form the centre of coil. Continue d s, drawing shuttle thread tight enough to make coil, with thumb and finger as sts are made, work three rows of d s from centre of coil, then one row, having a p after each third d s, cut threads, hold coil firmly and with fine thread sew ends on under side of coil, and around coil to hold rows in place.

The two coils nearest the body should have four rows before the p row to make them larger.

SMALLER WINGS. —Make 2 coils like those for larger wings, but continue with the stem, which leads from them through centre of wings thus: After sewing the coils in; ch 6 *half* sts like the first half of a d s, p, and 6 half sts like the *last* half of a d s. Continue until long enough to reach end of wings next to body. With a little help from thumb and finger the p thus made will fall alternately on each side of the centre, making a pretty double p cord. Now lap and fasten ends of wires of both pairs of wings. Sew coils to position by their

47

p to crocheted covering of wire on under side.

The ch of r from coils on edge of the large wings to centre coils, are made as follows: With shuttle thread make r of 2 d s, 17 p separated by 1 d s, 2 d s, close, make lock-stitch at close of each r thus: Draw loop of shuttle thread under ball thread, pass shuttle through loop, draw close, carry thread through centre of r just made on under side of r and join to centre p of same r. Proceed as before, making 4 r, each 2 p smaller than the one preceding. Make six of these chs of rs, sew the ends to centre coils, and also coils to edge of wings as illustrated.

Make two more chs of rs as follows: String a quantity of small jet beads on shuttle thread; r of 2 d s, 4 p separated by 2 d s, 2 d s, slipping a bead into each p as made, on one side of r, also as many beads as will fill the thread through centre of r. Join these jetted r to coil in lower corner of large wings, and to wired edge in form of ¼ circle. Make two separate r for each wing to fill open spaces and sew to position. Also with fine thread tack lightly across ch of rs on under side to hold in place.

Fasten sets of wings together by placing where wires are lapped, sew to under side of body.

ANTENNÆ.— These are made in same manner as the coils, having a black bead on thread at beginning, and drawing shuttle thread just tight enough to make them curve naturally.

FIG. 116. BAG WITH CORONATION CORD. SEE FIG. 110 AND PAGE 48

Figure 116. Bag with Coronation Cord. — Two balls crochet cotton No. 30 and three bunches of coronation cord are used (see Fig. 110, page 46).

WHEEL IN CENTRE. — Cut 72 sections of cord. *Outer row around wheel.*—* R 3 d s, p, 3 d s, join to a loop of cord, 3 d s, p, 3 d s. Ch 3 d s, p. 2 d s, p, 3 d s. Repeat from *, joining rings together, and to the sections of cord.

Inner row —* R 3 d s, p, 2 d s, join to cord, 1 d s,

join cord, 2 d s, p, 3 d s. Ch 2 d s, p, 2 d s; repeat from *. SMALL WHEELS.—Cut 30 sections of cord, 1 d s, join cord, * 2 d s, join cord. Repeat from * 13 times, 1 d s, close. There will be 15 loops of cord. Around this make a row of loops and chs; r 3 d s, p, 3 d s, join to cord, 3 d s, p, 3 d s; ch 4 d s, p, 2 d s, p, 4 d s. Join rings to cord and sew ends of cord to 2d p of last r. Join p on last 3 chs to ps of ch on large wheel (w). Join small ws together by 3 chs. Make 9 small ws. HALF WHEEL AT TOP CORNER.—Cut 14 sections of cord. Make same as small ws, forming into a half w and joining to two small ws at corner. Finish top of half w with 5 chs. Repeat at the other corner. This makes one side of bag. EDGE.—R 6 d s, p, 6 d s. Ch 6 d s, join to p in ch of w, 2 d s, join to next p in ch of w, 6 d s; repeat r twice, joining together. Alternate the rs and chs around the top. Repeat, joining rs of this row to those of last row, so as to make groups of four rs between chs. CORD. —Take seven 3½-yard lengths of cotton, twist tightly, double and twist again.

Border Design. —On page 21, Fig. 48, is one - half square used in pillow, Fig. 47, which shows a section of a border design. Make ½ of the square as directed for the pillow, and at the corners ¾ths. At the end of row 1, instead of "repeat ch," ch 5 d s, 3 p 3 d s between (bet), 5 d s, and continue with row 2. After last *, ch 5 d s, 3 p 3 d s bet, 5 d s and join base of centre r. *3d row*—Begins with r 7 d s, join first r at left of a daisy, 7 d s; ch 3 d s, 2 p 2 d s bet, 3 d s, join 1st p next ch, continue as in directions. This row joins the sections, and may be continued entirely around them. At the corner a third daisy is added to the two which form a section; and the centre has 3 r only to correspond in number. BORDER as on squares of pillow, except to join added daisy the ch is 3 d s, 5 p 2 d s bet, 3 d s; and it joins sections with a short ch at the inner side to connect with the joining border.

48

THE END